Catering:
Food Preparation
and Service

Catering: Food Preparation and Service

Ursula Jones, MHCIMA Cert. Ed.

Department of Catering and Hairdressing
Tresham College, Northamptonshire

Illustrated by Norman Laing NDD ATD

Edward Arnold

©URSULA J. JONES 1986

First published in Great Britain 1986 by
Edward Arnold (Publishers) Ltd, 41 Bedford Square, London WC1B 3DQ

Edward Arnold (Australia) Pty Ltd, 80 Waverley Road, Caulfield East,
Victoria 3145, Australia

British Cataloguing in Publication Data

Jones, Ursula
  Catering: food preparation and service.
  1. Caterers and catering.
  I. Title
  642'.4   TX943

  ISBN 0-7131-7493-5

To Frank and Barbara Ware

Text set in 11 on 12 Compugraphic Palacio
by Mathematical Composition Setters Limited, Salisbury, UK
Printed and bound in Great Britain by Richard Clay (The Chaucer Press) Ltd.,
Bungay, Suffolk

Contents

Preface

Catering: Food Preparation and Service has been written to fill an obvious need for a basic theory book, which is in an easily-read format, to encourage all students who have previously experienced difficulty with comprehension of the written word. It is aimed at those students who are, in any way, interested in, or studying, catering, either at their place of work, at a college of further education, or at a school. The extensive use of flow charts, diagrams, tables and illustrations is intended to increase the student's ability to understand and learn the theory element.

This catering book has been designed so that any topic being studied is easily found, and so that the relevant information, charts and illustrations are adjacent to the main text. Much of the information has been included in list or chart form to minimise the amount of written text. Brief descriptions of dishes are included for theoretical purposes and are not intended to be used as working recipes.

To help teachers there are questions in the form of assessment activities, which will extend the students' knowledge and their ability to apply this to their place of work or training. These activities have been designed so that the students may work as individuals or with two or three other students to form small groups.

Students studying skill/craft-based courses examined by the City and Guilds London Institute will find the contents relevant to examinations 706/1, 705, and the 700 skill series. Trainees studying HCITB and YTS craft proficiency training courses will find the book helpful and relevant to their training, as will those on TVEI and CPVE courses.

It is hoped that students will find the contents of this book interesting, useful and easy to understand. The subject of catering conjures up all manner of different types, sizes, styles and standards of establishments and services. I have endeavoured to give the reader an indication of the many principles involved, thereby equipping them to study any part of the catering industry in more depth as their career and studies progress.

This Food Services book contains basic information on food preparation, production and service, and the companion volume, *Catering: Housekeeping and Front Office* contains information concerned with house-keeping, hotel reception and the control of catering premises. These two books are intended to provide the necessary basic theoretical knowledge for catering students and should be used in conjunction with one another, together with practical skill instruction.

Thanks to my family and friends for their support and encouragement during the preparation of this book, and to P. Grundy, MHCIMA, DMF, for encouragement and technical advice.

Catering: Housekeeping and Front Office

The contents of this companion volume include:
residential establishments and staffing
the uses of various types of cleaning equipment and cleaning
agents
cleaning methods, standards, rotas and specifications
hospital cleanliness
choice and care of furniture, fittings and fabrics
types of floors
inspection and maintenance procedures
building safety and security
guests' bookings
reception and control procedures
billing control methods
communication methods
marketing principles
financial control.

Unit 1:

Catering Methods and Equipment

Methods of heat transference
Methods of cookery
The selection of catering equipment
Kitchen surfaces
Steamers and bains-marie
Catering ovens and ranges
Boiling tables, pans and bratt pans
Fryers, counter units and grills
Refrigerators
Deep freezers
Assessment activities

Transference of Heat

Heat is essential to cooking. It may be transferred by radiation, conduction, or convection. A fourth way of cooking is by microwave.

Radiation: Here heat passes from its source in direct rays until it falls on an object in its path. This is what happens when food is grilled.

Conduction: This happens when heat is transferred through a solid object by contact with that object. Conduction is the principle involved in the use of a solid electric or gas hot plate.

Convection: This is the movement of heated particles of gases and liquids. On heating, the particles expand, become less dense and rise. The colder particles sink to take their place, thus causing convection currents which distribute heat. Convection is the principle involved in the heating of an oven and in the heating of liquids.

Microwave: When the food is placed in the microwave oven, and the power is switched on, energy waves cause friction in the molecules of food and heat is generated. The cooking time is greatly reduced, and the shrinkage and moisture loss is minimal.

Microwaves are high-frequency electromagnetic waves similar to radio waves. They are generated by a vacuum tube called the magnetron, which converts electrical energy to microwave energy and then transfers it to the oven where it cooks the food.

Microwaves are reflected by metal, therefore it is not possible to cook with any metal containers. However, microwaves do pass through containers that are made of paper, high density plastic, china, and glass materials, with no ill-effect. As heat is produced within the food itself, only the food gets hot — the surrounding container and the air inside the oven remain cold. Microwaves penetrate food surfaces to a depth of several centimetres from all angles and start the rapid heating activity of the water, fat and sugar molecules. Because the heat is conducted below the surface, the food remains moist, not dry, and crisp.

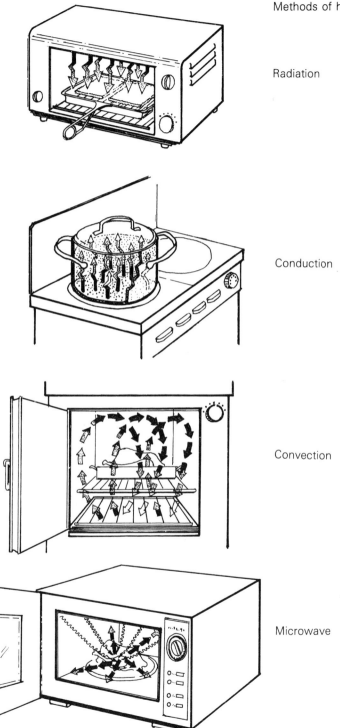

Methods of heat transference

Radiation

Conduction

Convection

Microwave

Methods of Cooking

Method	Description	Examples of veg/fruit	Examples of protein foods
Boiling	Cooking in a liquid in a pan with a well-fitting lid	Vegetables of the root, tuber, leaf groups	Silverside Leg of mutton Collar bacon
Simmering	Gentle cooking in liquid in a pan with a well-fitting lid	Vegetables of the flower group Vegetable soups	Meat, soups, Whole fish
Poaching	Gentle cooking in minimum liquid, just less than boiling	Asparagus, globe artichoke Fruits of the stone, soft and hard groups Rhubarb	Portions of fish Salmon Eggs
Steaming	*In container over boiling water *Steamer, minimum pressure 1¼ kg/cm^2 *High pressure steamer	Apples, rhubarb, potatoes, beetroot. Small quantities of frozen vegetables (high pressure steamer)	Meat puddings Whole fish
Stewing	Gentle simmering in lidded dish — moderate oven	Mixed vegetable dishes	Meat stews Casseroles Fish stews
Braising	Slow cooking on mirepoix of root vegetables in oven, minimum liquid in lidded dish	Celery, onions Fondant potatoes Savoury potatoes	Ox-liver Chicken Beef-olives Middle-neck of lamb

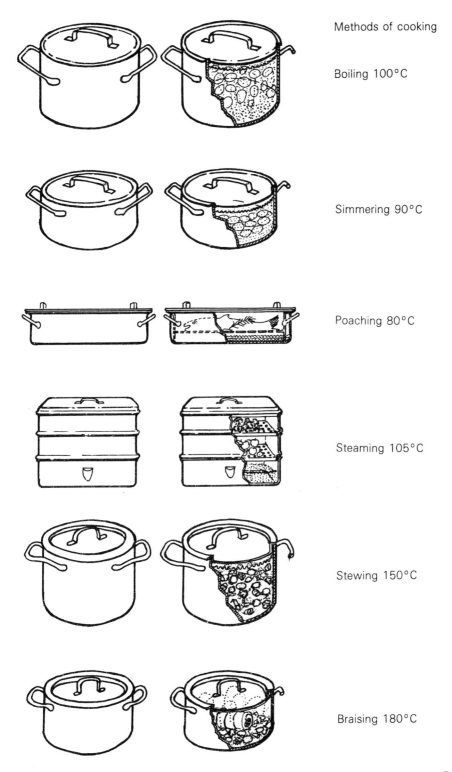

Methods of cooking

Boiling 100°C

Simmering 90°C

Poaching 80°C

Steaming 105°C

Stewing 150°C

Braising 180°C

Roasting (oven)

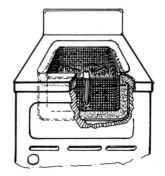

Deep frying

Shallow frying

Sautéing

Method	Description	Examples of veg/fruit	Examples of protein foods
Pot roasting	Joint cooked on base of root vegetables in a covered container, basted while cooking	—	Good quality joints of meat and poultry
Roasting	Cooked in tin, joint raised on bones/trivet, basted while cooking	Potatoes Parsnips Onions	Good quality joints of meat and poultry
Baking	Cooked in the oven in dry heat	Potatoes Apples Pears	Egg-custards
Grilling	Cooked over heat, under heat, or between heat	Tomatoes Potato dishes finished off	Small portions best quality meat and fish
Deep frying	Hot fat in deep fryer	Potatoes Fruit fritters	Coated meat Coated fish
Shallow frying	Minimum fat in shallow pan	Onions Mushrooms	Offal, bacon, sausages, fish
Sautéing	Tossed over heat, minimum fat	Potatoes Onions	Small meat portions, kidneys

The Selection of Catering Equipment

The following points should be considered:

- Space available — the size and height of the equipment.
- The cost — to purchase the equipment or lease.
- Sub–floor — sufficient strength in the floor to take the weight of the equipment.
- Energy supply — existing fuel supply able to take increased load.
- Drainage/water — adequate and suitable facilities, meter costs.
- Frequency of use — will the menu make good use of the equipment?
- Load/capacity — the equipment should be able to cook the quantities of food required by the normal menu.
- Time available — the equipment should be able to cook the food in the time available.

- Heat-up time — the length of time required to bring the equipment up to heat.
- Ease of use — the equipment should be easy for the staff to handle and control efficiently.
- Ease of maintenance — the equipment should be easy to clean and maintain.
- Additional equipment — is it necessary to use any additional equipment or attachments?
- Extraction — is it necessary to use an extraction system for fumes/steam?
- Noise — is the equipment likely to create an unacceptable noise level?
- Fuels — a large variety of catering equipment is available that may be operated by gas, electricity or solid fuel.
  — the choice between the fuels is governed by the actual fuel supply being available and the estimated fuel consumption making any increase in fuel use possible.

When the above points have been considered, check the following details to ensure that the best possible choice is made:

- The weight and solidness of construction.
- The ability to obtain spare parts and replacement parts.
- The handles, knobs, and switches should all be robust and heat resistant.
- The existing cooking equipment should be of a suitable size and weight to enable continued use.
- The staff should be capable of using the equipment properly.

Kitchen Surfaces

Type	Uses	Care	Equipment
Wood	Chopping blocks Chopping boards Rolling pins Spoons/spatulas	Carefully remove food debris. Wash with warm detergent water. Dry away from direct heat.	Wire brush Detergent with a sterilizer Cloth
Stainless steel gloss/matt	Sinks, splash guards Tables, shelves Trays, bowls Hotplates, ranges Ovens, grills Water boilers	Brush away or soak off any food debris, do not scratch the surface. Wash with detergent solution, or cream cleanser, rinse, dry.	Soft brush, plastic scraper, cloth Detergent with sterilizer Dry cloth

Type	Uses	Care	Equipment
Enamelled steel	Refrigerator cabinets Ranges, ovens	Wash with hot detergent water. Rinse. Dry. Do not scratch surface.	Cloth Detergent with sterilizer Dry cloth
Steel	Baking trays/sheets Oven shelves Ranges Hot plates	Wipe clean while still hot. Oil sparingly to avoid rusting.	Damp cloth Kitchen paper roll and edible oil
Cast iron	Frying pans Griddle plates Pans	Wash with hot detergent water. Rinse. Dry. Do not scratch/scrape surface.	Nylon brush. Dry and wet cloths Detergent with sterilizer
Chromium	Handles on equipment Runged shelves in oven Refrigerator shelves	Wash with hot detergent water. Soak to remove food stains.	Neutral detergent Soft cloths, wet and dry
Aluminium	Pans, trays Cooking equipment	Scouring powder and wire wool with hot water. Soak stains. Rinse well.	Scouring powder/pad, wire wool. Stiff brush. Detergent with sterilizer
Plastics	Handles on equipment Light equipment — bowls, chopping boards, shelves, work surfaces	Soak off any food debris. Wash in hot water with detergent. Rinse well. Dry.	Neutral detergent and soft brush Wet and dry cloths

Steamers and Bains-marie

Steamers

Areas of use:
- Where moist cooking methods are required;
- Industrial, commercial and welfare catering units;
- Where small quantities of food need to be moist-cooked, either in standard time or fast time.

Maintenance:
- Heat supply should be turned off;
- All trays and containers should be cleaned free from all grease and food particles;
- The water chamber should be cleaned and re-filled with clean water;
- The door should be left slightly open to allow free ventilation.

Design options:
- Atmospheric steamer — pressureless steamer; foods may be removed when cooked without harming other items still being cooked.
  - small quantities of different foods may be cooked in different trays at the same.
- Pressure steamer — foods are all cooked under pressure. A pressure safety valve regulates the cooking.
  - suitable for steaming large quantities of foods of a similar type at the same time.
- High compression steamer — this is suitable for defrosting and cooking small quantities of foods in half the normal time.
  - suitable for restaurant production where a variety of foods are required in small quantities in a short space of time.

Bain-marie hot plate

Areas of use:
- Cafeteria type of food service areas;
- Staggered food service times.

Maintenance:
- Heat supply turned off, water and food removed;
- All containers and shelves cleaned and replaced;
- Whole unit cleaned outside and inside, doors left open.

Design options:
  - may be steam, water or electric elements to heat foods.
  - choice of top containers available, including carving trays and containers that may be used in the oven or steamer when cooking the foods.
  - display shelf with infra-red lamps.
  - cold display food areas, chilled holding cabinets.

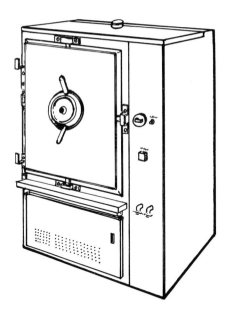

Industrial steaming oven

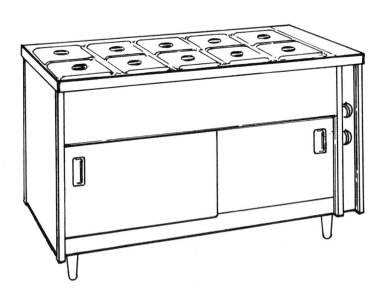

Bain-marie hot plate

Catering Ovens and Ranges

Ovens

Areas of use:
- Where large quantities of foods are to be either roasted or baked at the same time;
- Used in large-scale production areas in commercial and welfare catering establishments.

Maintenance:
- Turn off heat supply;
- Clean inside oven if required and check drip trays;
- Clean any glass vision areas and light screens;
- Clean exterior surfaces, including the top and the legs.

Design options:
- — multi-deck units with a combination of roast or bake ovens are available.
- — sections may be provided with an oven vent.
- — interior light in bake/pastry ovens.
- — racks in roast ovens, and may be used in bake ovens too.
- — steam injection for pastry ovens may be installed.
- Forced air convection — more foods may be cooked at the same time, using multiple racks.
  - — hot air is circulated by a fan, reducing the cooking time.
  - — rack of trayed products may be rolled into the oven and rolled out again on the same rack when cooked.
- Cook and hold — slow cooking at a low temperature and, after a pre-set time, turns automatically to hold temperature at 200°C, used for roasting to minimise shrinkage of the meat.
  - — useful for an à la carte menu to keep roasts at their best.
- Convection and microwave — combines forced air convection and microwave energy, giving increased speed of cooking with traditional colour and texture.
- Integrated convection, grill and microwave oven — combines forced air convection, microwave and grill to give maximum selection of cooking methods within the same unit.
  - — useful in small à la carte menu units or extensive bar snack trade kitchens where each order is individually cooked.
  - — a very quick method of cooking small items effectively.

General purpose ranges

Areas of use:
- Heaviest cooking demands, when baking and boiling facilities are required;

- Hotels, hospitals, schools, large cafeterias, restaurants;
- When limited floor space is available.

Maintenance:
- Turn off heat supply when not in use;
- Clean gas jets, and all removable parts and replace;
- Clean all drip trays, grease troughs, and backguards.

Design options — Tops:
Backguard — fitted to protect wall and to prevent pans being accidently pushed back too far.
Solid top — to facilitate the use of large and small pans.
   — to ensure even heat distribution. Long slow cooking at the edges of the solid top.
   — the centre may be removed for direct heat contact.
Open burners, gas — various diameters are available to suit all sizes of pans that may be used.
Castors — available on smaller models to make cleaning and maintenance easier.
Griddle top — solid fry surface fitted with splash guards and grease trough.

Design options — Ovens:
Door — may be hinged at the base, side-hinged or double side-hinged to accommodate all kitchen sizes and designs.
Shelves — adjustable heights are available. Solid sheet or rungs.
Heat — standard or fan assisted.
   — thermostatically controlled.
Cleaning — porcelain enamel coating inside the oven enables the walls to clean themselves continually by the action of heat upon the surface.

Industrial convection oven and rack on wheels

Boiling Tables, Pans and Bratt Pans

Boiling tables

Areas of use:
• Where additional boiling/simmering facilities are required.
Maintenance:
• Turn off energy supply and check gas jets;
• Clean drip tray, base tray and stand.
Design options:
• Height — may be single burner size, with low level for stock pot
  use.
  — may be same height as other surfaces in the unit.
•Burners — may choose number and size suitable for production
  use.
•Storage — open shelves or cupboard space beneath, to store
  equipment.
•Backguard — may be fitted for increased safety and hygiene.

Boiling pans

Areas of use:
• Where large quantities of foods need to be boiled or simmered at
  the same time for bulk service;
• Used in large cafeterias, hospitals, prisons.
Maintenance:
• Turn off energy supply, check gas jets, turn off water supply;
• Clean thoroughly inside and outside. Leave lid ajar;
• Check tilting mechanism, and drainage tap;
• Clean under pans and their support stands.
Design options:
  — capacity from 10 litre to 40 litre size.
  — steam outer jacket to facilitate even cooking without burning.
  — tilting device for easy emptying and cleaning.
  — base drainage tap for easy cleaning.
  — mains water tap for easy filling and cleaning.
  — interior mesh vegetable basket for easy drainage of cooked
    vegetables.

Bratt pans

Areas of use:
• Where large quantities of foods are to be shallow fried, braised,
  stewed or poached;
• Used in large-scale welfare catering establishments.
Maintenance:
• Turn off heat supply,
• Clean inside taking care not to scratch the surface,
• Clean outside, underneath, and support legs,
• Leave lid ajar and check the tilting mechanism.

Design options:
— one base pedestal, or may be housed in solid side panels.
— varying internal cooking capacity.
— small size with lift device instead of tilting mechanism.

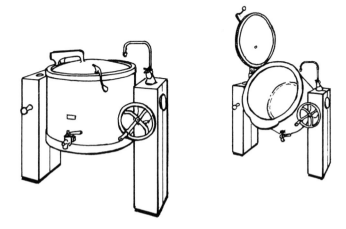

Boiling pan (tilting pattern)

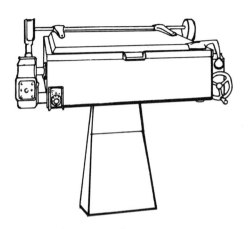

Bratt pan (tilting pattern)

Fryers, Counter Units and Grills

Fryers

Areas of use:
- Where deep-fried foods are prepared regularly;
- Commercial, industrial, and welfare catering units.

Maintenance:
- The heat supply should be turned off;
- The oil/fat should be drained out and filtered, to remove particles of fried food;
- The frying chamber should be cleaned and all the grease marks removed;
- All surrounding inside and outside areas need to be cleaned.

Design options:
- — thermostatically-controlled frying chamber.
- — timer for perfect frying results. No over-cooking.
- — automatic basket lifts, pre-set cooking time, computerized.
- — computer-operated banks of fryers to cope with multi-product menu.
- — swing out heating elements for easy cleaning.
- — high back and side splash guards.

Counter units

Areas of use:
- Where small quantities of snack/basic call order type foods are cooked and served direct to the customer;
- Used in small restaurants, snack bars, cafés, bars.

Maintenance:
- The heat supply should be turned off;
- Each component part should be cleaned thoroughly, all removable parts cleaned, and gas jets checked;
- Splash backs, drip trays, and grease troughs must be washed and cleared of grease.

Design options:
- — space is kept to a minimum to allow the maximum number of units to be included in any one site.
- — units can be banked both front and rear by using a banking plate, so making one continuous row of units.
- — the counter may comprise any combination of the following units:

sandwich griddle	food warmer
griddle	hot plate
fryer	grill
pizza oven	high pressure steamer
convection oven	microwave oven
chilled cupboard	refrigerator

Grills and salamanders

Areas of use:
- Where it is necessary for foods to be cooked quickly;
- When browning or a toasted finish is needed.

Maintenance:
- The heat supply should be turned off;
- All cooking bars, racks, sheets, and trays should be cleaned free from grease after use;
- The base drip tray and grease trough should be emptied and cleaned;
- The inside area of the grill chamber should be cleaned, all splash marks from fat must be removed;
- The top, back and sides, including the supports, should be cleaned.

Design options:
- Grills — variable heat settings are available.
  - heat may be from above the food or from underneath the food.
  - double-sided or contact grills enable the food to be cooked with heat from above and below at the same time.
- Broilers — solar-ray gives economy of fuel consumption and infra-red burners.
  - radiant heat broiler is suitable for multi-product cooking in large quantities.
  - char-broiler combines the burning of the meat juices with a flare control blower to create the popular char flavour to foods.
  - infra-red broiler is ideal for au gratin work for browning foods.

Equipment safety

The following points need to be considered:
- Adequate staff training is necessary before equipment is used.
- Staff should be tall enough to use equipment safely — grills are often high.
- Waste food particles will burn easily and may ignite if not removed.
- Splashes of grease and fat may ignite if not cleaned away.
- Drip trays and grill troughs need to be kept clean, to prevent fire.
- Large trays will be heavy and hot, care is needed when removing them from the oven.
- The tops of grills, salamanders, ovens and steamers have air vents which must be kept clear and clean.
- The tops of equipment are often hot — nothing must be placed on these surfaces.
- Solid top ranges may be switched off but the heat will be retained for a considerable length of time.

- Gas safety taps must always be switched off when equipment is not in use.
- Drainage water taps may be hot and will splash when opened.
- Electricity switches should be off when equipment is not in use.

Refrigerators

A refrigerator is a cabinet with well lagged walls and a door which closes tightly to insulate the inside. Inside, an evaporator surrounds a smaller compartment used for ice-making. The evaporator absorbs heat from the foods and the whole compartment. In doing so it sets up convection currents in the air enclosed in the cabinet and also draws moisture out of the foods. This moisture condenses and forms frost on the outside of the evaporator.

Using a refrigerator
- Open the door as seldom as is possible.
- Arrange foods so that the air can circulate, so that convection currents can be set up to draw the heat from the food and pass it up to the evaporator.
- Keep all food covered to prevent it from becoming dried as the heat is extracted from it, and to prevent smells and odours passing from one type of food to another. If food is left uncovered it produces an extra amount of moisture and then frost, which reduces the efficiency of the refrigerator.
- All foods placed in the refrigerator should be in clean containers and be cold.
- One person should have the responsibility of checking the contents of the refrigerator on a daily basis; it must never be used to keep foods that are stale and unwanted.

Cleaning a refrigerator
1 Switch off and remove all contents. Put food in cold place, covered and off the floor.
2 Leave a deep tray under the evaporator and prop open the door.
3 Remove all shelves, wash them thoroughly, rinse well, and stand them up to enable them to dry properly.
4 Wash shelf brackets and any fixed shelves inside the refrigerator. Rinse well.
5 Wipe all inside walls to remove any food particles, dry well.
6 When all the ice has slipped from the evaporator, wipe well and dry.

7 Clean the floor area, rinse well and dry.
8 When everything is dry, replace all the shelves and the trays.
9 Close the door and switch on the power. Check that the motor is running.
10 Clean the outside of the refrigerator, paying particular attention to the handles and the top surface.
11 When the inside is at the required temperature, i.e. less than 2°C, replace all the food as quickly as possible.

Deep Freezers

Food that is frozen remains preserved indefinitely; freezing is not only the best method of preserving foods, it is the simplest. Bacteria which cause food poisoning, and cause foods to deteriorate, are made inactive at −18°C. When foods are commercially deep frozen they are taken down to a temperature of −22°C.

Use of a deep freeze

- Never put any foods in until they are absolutely cold.
- Always label foods and keep a record of products in the deep freeze.
- Check the interior temperature at regular intervals and have the freezer serviced regularly.
- When buying commercially frozen foods transfer them to your deep freeze as soon as they are delivered.
- Never re-freeze food once it has been thawed out unless it has been cooked, as for example, frozen sausage meat, thawed and made into sausage rolls, and then placed in the deep freeze without cooking first — bacteria will multiply all the time the sausage meat is out of the freezer. The sausage rolls may be made and then cooked, and only then will it be safe to re-freeze them.
- Carefully pack portioned foods, such as steaks, so that it will be possible to take them from the deep freeze, one at a time, not all in a solid block.
- Ready-cooked casserole type foods freeze well; but always freeze in a quantity that may be re-used conveniently.
- Bread products may be frozen successfully, and are useful in emergencies. Sandwiches freeze well, with the one exception of those filled with eggs. Store sandwiches by the loaf, uncut and with the crusts on.
- Cakes freeze well if adequately wrapped and boxed, sliced or uncut items are useful.
- Pastry may be frozen either raw, in 500g packs wrapped in foil or polythene, or in its cooked state ready to be finished off as required.

Defrosting foods

All food should be adequately thawed out before cooking. (Frozen vegetables are the only exception.) It should be placed in the refrigerator on a clean tray and allowed to defrost slowly. If heat is applied to the frozen food the outer layers will thaw and then begin to cook before the interior part has even had a chance to thaw out; this will cause increased bacterial growth, and food poisoning may result.

Foods	Time in refrigerator
Vegetables	Cook from frozen
Fruit	6 hours
Fish	6–8 hours
Joints of meat	8 hours per 2 kg weight
Sausages, chops	6 hours
Cooked casseroles	10–15 hours
Poultry	24 hours per 5kg weight

See also pages 122–3.

Unit 1 Assessment Activities

1. (a) List items of catering equipment at your place of work or training.
   (b) Describe their main function and uses.
   (c) Note the method of heat transfer used in each item of equipment.
   (d) List the safety factors that apply to each piece of equipment.

2. (a) Describe types of foods that may be successfully prepared in a microwave oven.
   (b) Test one recipe by cooking half the quantity by traditional methods and half by using the microwave oven.
   (c) Compare the results by paying particular attention to the following: texture; colour; consistency; time taken; flavour; cost of fuel.

3. (a) Compare a domestic-type cooker with a heavy duty catering range.
   (b) Discuss the reasons for the differences between the two items of equipment.

4. (a) Compile a cleaning schedule for a kitchen at your place of work or training.
   (b) Include the large items of equipment and the small light equipment.
   (c) Describe exactly how one item of large equipment should be cleaned.

5. (a) Draw a scale outline plan of a kitchen that you work in and re-plan the interior fittings and equipment.
   (b) Indicate the type of equipment that you have selected, giving reasons for your choice.
   (c) Describe the surfaces and finishes that you have selected, giving reasons for your choice.

Unit 2:

Light Meals and Beverages

Hors d'oeuvres
Chilled beverages
Canapés and savouries
Sandwiches
Hot snacks
Breakfast service
Coffee
Tea
Assessment activities

Hors d'Oeuvres

Hors d'oeuvres are served as an appetising start to the meal. They stimulate the gastric juices and therefore aid the digestion. They are highly flavoured colourful foods, served together in small portions. Creating hors d'oeuvres can be a way of incorporating different foods and textures into the menu and useful for eliminating the wastage of small amounts of foods.

Single food hors d'oeuvres

These are already plated or portioned in an appropriate dish or glass. They are ready to eat and are neatly presented and garnished. A doily and an under-plate should be placed under the dish.

Plate:
Smoked salmon
Carved thinly, decorated with sprigs of parsley and lemon wedges. Brown bread and butter served separately.

Liver pâté
Pâté cut into slices and placed on lettuce leaves. Decorated with sliced cucumber and tomato.
Toast is served separately, usually cut into fingers.

Salami sausage
Thin slices are arranged so that they overlap on a bed of lettuce, garnished with sprigs of parsley.

Sardines
These are boned and trimmed, then placed onto a bed of lettuce. They are garnished with slices of cucumber.

Potted shrimps
The shrimps are separated and placed on a heart of lettuce. They are garnished with a wedge of lemon and sprigs of parsley.

Liver pâté and lemon wedge

Dish:

Chilled Melon
A thick slice is cut and the flesh is cut into even-sized pieces; this cut flesh is left on the skin. The melon is served chilled, garnished with orange slices and a maraschino cherry.
Ground ginger and caster sugar are served separately.

Grapefruit
The fruit is halved, the flesh loosened, and a cherry is placed in the centre core area. It is served chilled in a glass dish or coupe. Caster sugar is served from a sugar sifter.

Grapefruit and Orange Cocktail
Prepared segments are placed in a coupe dish or a glass. They are decorated with a cherry and served chilled.

Florida Cocktail
A mixture of prepared grapefruit, pineapple and orange segments is placed in cocktail glasses. The cocktail glass may be sugared around the rim. It is served chilled.

Fruit Cocktail
Mixed fruits are prepared and cut to even-sized pieces, soaked in a light lemon-flavoured syrup, then piled into cocktail glasses, and served chilled.

Melon Cocktail
The flesh of ripe melon is scooped out with a ball cutter. The balls are then served in glass dishes, chilled well.

Avocado Pear
Ripe halved stoned pear is placed in a dish and garnished with lettuce hearts and shrimps; it is usually sprinkled with a light vinaigrette dressing just before service.

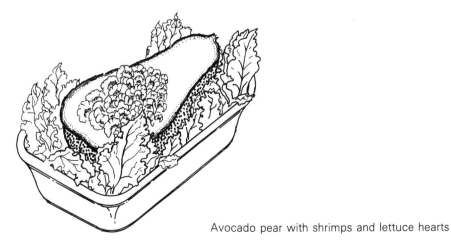

Avocado pear with shrimps and lettuce hearts

Service of assorted hors d'oeuvres

These are dressed in raviers or small glass dishes and placed on an hors d'oeuvre trolley. If there is no trolley available, or the amount of hors d'oeuvres is small, they may be prepared and served from round or rectangular segmented hors d'oeuvre trays.

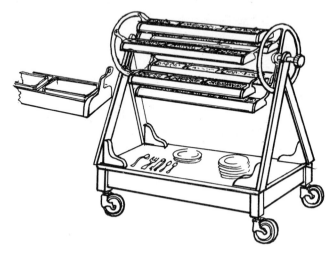

Hors d'oeuvres trolley

These assorted hors d'oeuvres are selected by the customer in the restaurant and served from the tray or trolley onto a 20cm plate by the waiter. The waiter uses clean serving utensils for each type of hors d'oeuvre and arranges the selected items tastefully upon the plate. The plates and service utensils are stacked on a shelf on the lower part of the trolley. As an individual ravier becomes empty it may be replaced by a fresh one by the waiter, thus ensuring a continuous selection of items for future customers, and an attractive display upon the trolley at all times.

Chilled Beverages

Chilled fruit juices are sometimes served in place of an hors d'oeuvre. They are served in attractive 125ml glasses placed on a 10cm plate with a patterned doily.

The juice should be of a distinctive colour and flavour so that its origin is easily recognisable to the customer. It should be smooth in texture and chilled. It should never be thick in consistency or too sweet.

26

Juices may be prepared upon order with an electrical juice extractor or purchased already prepared in one of the following forms:

Tinned: Ready to drink. Various sizes of tin available.
Bottled: Ready to drink. One portion per bottle, or a larger jar may be purchased, for dispensing as required.
Dehydrated: This is in fine granular form and is mixed with water as required. It may be purchased in bulk per litre or in individual sachets. Chilled water should be used, the powder dissolves when briskly stirred into the water.
Frozen: This is purchased in one-portion sized cans. The flavour is excellent but the thawing time required makes it of limited commercial use.
Fresh in cartons: These are fresh whole fruit juices that have been packed into vacuum-sealed sterile cartons. The juice contains no preservative and so the shelf life is limited.

Types of juices

Orange: Serve with a slice of orange over the rim of the glass.
Pineapple: Serve with a fresh mint leaf and shredded pineapple placed in the glass.
Grapefruit: Serve with a slice of lemon over the rim of the glass.
Apple: Serve with a fresh mint leaf and a slice of apple in the glass.
Tomato: Serve with Worcester sauce offered separately.
Mixed tropical: Serve in a tall glass with two or more types of fruit to garnish. A cube of ice should be placed in the base of the glass.

Canapés and Savouries

Canapés are served as appetisers before a meal to accompany aperitifs. They are placed in a neat and tidy way on large oval or circular trays and offered to guests as they sip their aperitifs and await the forthcoming meal.

Canapés are based on neat slices of white or brown bread, toasted and cut into small squares, rectangles or circles. Each canapé is intended to be small enough for it to be eaten in one mouthful.

Selected neat slivers of meat or fish are arranged on each toasted base that has been spread with a complementary flavoured butter, for example, butter flavoured with horseradish with thin slivers of rare roast beef. These canapés are then creatively garnished with delicately cut vegetables and thinly glazed with aspic.

Assorted canapés

Substitutes for canapés

In many modern catering establishments, canapés are not served. The preparation time is very long and the type of service offered is not always compatible with such elaborate foods. Therefore the following substitutes are often offered to guests:

Potato Crisps: Various flavours may be purchased, either plain or crinkle cut. Keep airtight so that they remain crisp.
Potato sticks: May be potato-based or made from dehydrated potato products.
Savoury shapes: Made from deep-fried pasta shapes. Various flavours and shapes available.
Nuts: Salted peanuts, almonds and cashew nuts, or dry roasted nuts.
Nuts with Raisins: Whole nuts — almonds, hazels and Brazils, mixed with raisins.
Vegetables: White silverskin onions or small sweet pickled onions, gherkins and stuffed olives.

Savouries

Savouries are small tasty items that may be eaten in a few mouthfuls. They should be neatly garnished and have an attractive, appetising appearance. They are served between the sweet course and the cheese course on a full traditional menu.
Method of service: They are served very hot on a dish with a plain dish paper, and sprigs of parsley.
 : They are served by the waiter onto a hot 20cm plate for the guests. The savouries should be eaten with a small-sized knife and fork.

Purpose: They remove the sweetness left from the dessert course.
: They are useful for utilising small amounts of food.
: They create variety on the menu.

Small savouries may be created on many types of base, for example:
- Toast with crusts removed — Scotch Woodcock
  — Anchovy fillets
  — Devilled Kidneys
  — Welsh Rarebit
- Puff pastry bouchées — Shrimps or mixed shellfish
  — Chicken and ham in velouté sauce
- Puff or short paste barquettes — Devilled soft roes
  — Prawns in cream sauce

Other items may be served as a savoury or as a hot snack and may be made in individual sizes or portioned as required. These types of dishes are often served as incidental meals or supper items, either on their own or with salad foods and bread rolls. For example:

Soufflé: A panada béchamel, flavoured with cheese and eggs, baked in a hot oven until it is well risen, it must be served immediately.
Fritters: Flavoured with cheese or mushrooms. A yeast batter will ensure a crisp coating. These must be served immediately.
Flan: Egg custard based in either a short crust, puff paste or choux paste case. It may be flavoured with onions, ham, cheese, mixed herbs, fish, tomato, or any combination, to create an acceptable flavour and colour of filling. Flans must be cooked carefully to ensure that the pastry is properly cooked and that the egg-based filling is set without allowing it to curdle.
Croûtes: Thick slices of white bread, scooped out and fried, filled with a tasty filling such as cheese and tunny fish.

Sandwiches

Sandwiches are served in many different types of outlets and at various times of the day. They are used:

- As part of a traditional afternoon tea.
- Miniature sized, served as part of a finger buffet.
- As part of a pub lunchtime menu.
- At railway and motorway service areas.
- In vending machine sales.
- For retail sales from sandwich bars and shops.

Filled bread rolls are also served in increasing quantities and their advantages to the caterer are numerous:

29

- They need minimum preparation time and cause no wastage.
- They give good quality control and portion control.
- There is a large variety of shapes, types and flavours of bread rolls available to the caterer.
- They may be stored in a deep freeze unit and used as required.
- There is often a larger profit margin than on sandwiches, as rolls provide more bulk and take less filling.
- If they are wrapped in clingfilm, or placed in a disposable plastic type holder, they may be kept fresh for up to 24 hours as long as they are kept in a chilled counter.

Storage and service

- When filled and prepared, they should be wrapped in polythene or clingfilm or other see-through containers to ensure that they remain fresh and in a saleable form. They may be picked up by the customer without risks of contamination.
- If large quantities of sandwiches are prepared, the crusts should be trimmed as close to service time as possible to ensure freshness.
- If sandwiches or rolls are to be stored or frozen for any length of time, care should be taken when selecting the filling — egg and green salad items do not deep freeze successfully.
- Care should be exercised when selecting the fillings, one flavour should not dominate the remaining ingredients.
- Prepared rolls and sandwiches should be kept on refrigerated display units and the filling should be visible, so that there is no need to handle the item unnecessarily.

Types of bread and rolls

Bread: White — standard, farmhouse, low calorie.
    : Continental — French style, rye bread.
    : Brown or wheatmeal, wholemeal (wholewheat), granary, Hovis.
Rolls: Crusty — white, wholemeal, circular or long in shape.
    : Soft — white, wholemeal, granary, with poppy seeds.
    : Baps — white circular, bridge rolls, standard and small sized.

Fillings

There are many ways that rolls and sandwiches may be filled and seasoned, either by using just one main ingredient or a combination of ingredients to create more flavour and a variety of colours and textures.

Types of single fillings	Seasonings
Meat — sliced, pâté, paste	Mustard — English, mild
Fish — pâte, paste, shellfish	Mayonnaise, salad creams
Eggs — hard-boiled and creamed, scrambled	Salad creams, cress
Cheese — grated, sliced, spread, cottage	Pickle, chutney, dates
Salad — tomato, lettuce, cucumber, watercress, cress	Vinaigrette, black pepper, diced onion

Any of the single fillings may be combined with one or more of the salad items to create an attractive flavour. The use of combined fillings is often necessary as salad items do make an ordinary sandwich more interesting, and they can also be used to increase the number and types of sandwiches offered for sale without too many basic fillings being used.

Basic types of sandwiches

Toasted: By inserting a hot filling between two slices of hot buttered toast.

 : By making a sandwich and then toasting it using an electric sandwich toaster.

Double-decker: Made from three slices of bread, two white and one brown. Used to make a two-layered sandwich with two complementary fillings and giving a variety of colour. The sandwich is cut into rectangles or squares before being served.

Open: These are made onto a base of thick buttered slices of bread. Each slice is then topped with an attractive selection of meat or fish items and garnished neatly with salad commodities.

Open sandwich

Hot Snacks

These are served in many types of catering outlet and are not available at any definite time as conventional meals are; they are normally available as requested. The foods served are often based upon the traditional breakfast dishes, with modern and regional variations. Chipped potatoes are usually included in these meals.

Hot snacks may be either self-service or by waiter service and are served in the following types of outlets:
• school meals and industrial catering units,
• motorway service areas and transport cafés,
• cafés adjacent to shopping or commercial areas,
• departmental store restaurants,
• fish and chip restaurants and shops.

The following are examples of foods that may be included in such meals:

Deep fried — fish, chips, chicken, scampi, croquettes, fritters.

Shallow fried — sausages, bacon, eggs, omelets, bread, potatoes, onions.

Grilled — toast, toast snacks, tomatoes, mushrooms, fish.

Griddle — steak, chops, beefburgers, cheeseburgers, chickenburgers.

Baked — meat pies, pasties, flans, pizzas, potatoes — filled with cheese.

Boiled — peas, beans, baked beans, carrots.

Beverages — tea, coffee, soup, milk and milk drinks, fruit drinks.

Accompaniments include: sandwiches, bread rolls, cakes, biscuits, cold sweets, fruit pies, ice-creams and confectionery.

Methods of service

The majority of popular snack establishments are based on one of two methods — self-service and waitress service. The prime concern is speed of service and therefore the highest hourly percentage rate of table occupancy is essential for profitability. To achieve this, fast and efficient service must be complemented by adequate kitchen back-up and hot plate re-stocking procedures, as well as thorough, methodical table-clearing and cleaning staff. (See pages 182–3.)

Breakfast Service

Breakfast may be served by either of the following methods in hotels:

In the bedroom
• Orders are given by completing a card that is placed in the guest's room.

- The trays are laid up the night before and left in the room-service room ready for the morning.
- The food items and beverages are placed on the tray at the service time and the tray is then delivered to the room.

In the hotel restaurant
- The tables are laid and the sideboards prepared after the evening service is completed.
- In the morning the sideboard is laid with jugs of chilled fruit juice, bowls of compôte of fruits, and individual packets of breakfast cereals.
- The tables are laid with jugs of milk, pats of butter, pots of preserves, baskets of bread rolls and pastries.
- The guests help themselves from the sideboard.
- The food service personnel serve the pots of tea and coffee and racks of toast from the still room.
- The cooked part of the meal is collected by the food service personnel from the kitchen and served to the guest.

All breakfast service should be quick, quiet and efficient, as guests will have a fixed schedule and may be very easily upset at this time of the day. The restaurant should make good use of all natural daylight as guests will wish to read the daily newspapers and will not appreciate a dimly lit room first thing in the morning.

(See page 180 for other forms of service.)

Breakfast lay-up for one person

Coffee

Coffee is grown in countries within 25 degrees of the Equator. It is the seed of a fruit which grows on a flowering evergreen shrub, which is grown to a height of 2.5 metres. The fruit changes from green to red as it ripens.

Coffee is a mild stimulant, due to the presence of caffeine which provides a feeling of alertness. Ground coffee has no food value but instant coffee contains a very small quantity of protein, fat, iron, carbohydrate and calcium. Most of the coffee is now roasted to produce the characteristic flavour and aroma. For the best results, coffee beans should be ground just before use.

Quality

- Unless the coffee is ground finely enough the water will not extract all the soluble materials and some of the flavour will be lost.
- The flavour of coffee will deteriorate when it is in contact with the atmosphere. It should be stored in dry airtight containers, and used in controlled stock rotation to ensure freshness.
- It is essential to select the type of coffee that is suitable for the method used to make the coffee. Some coffee is ground extra finely for use in filter machines.
- Coffee may be prepared by filtering, percolating, or infusing the coffee with boiling water.

Types

Coffee bags: Ground coffee is sealed in bags that are designed to make either one cup of coffee or a quantity such as one litre or four litres. These bags ensure consistency of flavour, quality and cost for the unit.

Instant coffee: This is produced in powder or granular form and is manufactured from liquid coffee. It may be purchased in various sized containers or individual one-cup sachets.

It must be kept in dry airtight containers as it will rapidly lose its true flavour if left exposed to the atmosphere.

Coffee essence: This is sweetened concentrated liquid coffee used to prepare iced coffee or flavoured items made in the bakery, such as gâteau mocha.

Coffee grades: These include — Blue Mountain from Jamaica, Mysore from India, Turkish, Brazilian and Kenyan blends.

Blended French coffee contains chicory which extends the flavour of the beans and gives a distinctive strong taste.

Tea

Tea is obtained from the leaves of an evergreen shrub which grows readily on the hills of monsoon countries. It is blended in its country of origin.

Tea as a beverage is a mild stimulant because of its caffeine content. The flavour will deteriorate when the tea is in contact with the atmosphere, therefore stocks should be used in rotation. Loose tea or tea bags should be stored in airtight containers. It is not advisable to hold excessive stocks of tea as its flavour will deteriorate with time. It also absorbs flavours from other foods, so for this reason care must be taken with its storage.

Tea bags: Because of its convenience and the ease of portion control and quality control the tea bag is extensively used in the catering trade. The bags are made from special paper which is able to withstand the effects of boiling water. The tea bags contain fine grades of tea which produce excellent quality tea. They are manufactured in individual portion size as well as for a gallon of tea.

Instant tea: Vending machines that serve tea by the cup often use instant tea. It is reasonably successful in producing an acceptable taste and colour, but is not used in any significant quantities in any other outlets.

Blends of tea: Assam — a full-bodied tea from North-East India.

Ceylon — a high quality tea with a delicate flavour.

Darjeeling — a delicately flavoured tea from the Himalayas.

Earl Grey — a tea with a more pronounced flavour, blended from Darjeeling and China tea.

China — teas from China are mild in flavour, have a larger leaf size and are generally more expensive. They are often served for after-noon tea with milk or lemon.

Preparation of tea

- 60g of tea per 5 litres of boiling water or one teaspoon of tea per person, if using small teapots, will make an acceptable brew of tea.
- It is essential to use freshly boiled water.
- To increase the flavour a warmed pot or urn is recommended.
- It is necessary to allow the tea to brew or infuse before serving. Allow 3–4 minutes per teapot, or 5–6 minutes per tea urn.
- Some tea urns have a removable tea infusion canister which prevents the tea from becoming too strong before it is actually served to the customer.
- Fresh cold milk is usually added to the cup of tea, the quantity being left to the discretion of the customer. A slice of lemon rather than milk is sometimes added to China tea.
- White sugar is offered, either in cubes or granulated.

Unit 2 Assessment Activities

1. List and describe the preparation of foods that may be used on an hors d'oeuvre trolley.

2. (a) Compile a simple questionnaire to determine the popularity of non-alchoholic fruit-based drinks.
   (b) Complete this questionnaire for two different age groups of people, such as a group of teachers and a group of young people.
   (c) Plot the results on a bar chart.
   (d) Discuss the differences and preferences of the two groups.

3. (a) Describe and design a tray of canapés suitable for production by your class.
   (b) Each prepare one type of canapé from your choice.
   (c) Compare all the types of canapés that have been prepared by your class in terms of: texture; flavour; cost; appearance.

4. (a) Visit retail establishments in your area and list the types of sandwiches and filled rolls that are offered for sale.
   (b) Compare the results with the use of a graph or chart.
   (c) Note the price differences and the methods of packaging.

5. (a) Imagine that you are working in a seaside hotel where families of holiday-makers are staying for a week. Compile a set of 5 picnic menus that could be prepared by the hotel and given to these families to take out with them each day.
   (b) Give a costing for each of the 5 picnic menus.
   (c) Indicate the most appropriate method of packaging these picnics.

Unit 3:

Soups, Sauces, Farinaceous Foods, and Vegetables

Stocks
Soup
Sauces:
  Béchamel
  Velouté
  Espagnol
  Miscellaneous
Farinaceous foods and pasta
Rice and pasta dishes
Pulses
Classification of vegetables
Cooking and serving vegetables
Convenience vegetables
Vegetable cuts and terms
Potatoes
Potato dishes
Assessment activities

Stocks

Definition

A stock is a liquid containing some of the soluble nutrients and flavours of the ingredients, which are extracted by prolonged simmering.

There are three basic types of stock:

Brown — vegetables and bones are browned.

White — white meats.

Fish — cooked for 20 minutes only.

Proportions

The usual proportions are:

4 litres water

2 kg bones   ⎱ Browned if a brown

½ kg vegetables ⎰ stock is to be made

1 bouquet garni

12 peppercorns

Method

- Only fresh meat bones and vegetables should be used.
- Never keep adding to the stockpot once it has started cooking.
- The scum that rises to the top of the pot should be removed.
- Fat globules that float on the surface should be removed.
- The stock should be simmered gently, not boiled.
- No salt or pepper should be added while it is cooking.
- If the stock has to be kept, it should be strained, cooled quickly, then placed in a clean pot and put in the refrigerator.
- It is dangerous to keep stock for more than 24 hours.

Convenience stock products

There are two forms of ready-made stock: dehydrated — granules, powder or cubes; and concentrated — paste, essence.

The advantages of convenience stock products include the following:

- They are always available.
- They are easily mixed in large or small quantities.
- It is possible to have a standard flavoured product always available.
- Standard costings are available.
- Minimum risk of food poisoning if the stock does not have to be stored.
- Minimum preparation time.

Uses

Stocks can be used for:
- Soups
- Sauces
- Gravies
- Liquor for braising foods.

Soup

A good soup should:
- Be of a good recognisable flavour;
- Have seasoning which complements the main flavour;
- Be free from grease or scum;
- Have a good definite colour;
- Be of a definite consistency — not lumpy or too thick;
- Stimulate the digestive juices.

There are 5 categories of soup:

Soup	Description	Accompaniments
Consommé	A clear soup made from a good flavoured stock, cleared with careful skimming and straining procedures.	Specific garnishes, dependent upon the type of consommé
Broth	Made from good stock and diced vegetables, meat, and rice or pearl barley. The vegetables and cereals are not removed.	Chopped parsley sprinkled on top. Meat and cereals remain in the broth
Velouté	A soup made from blond roux and white stock. Finished with cream and egg yolk liaison.	Garnish dependent upon type of soup, e.g. diced chicken for chicken velouté
Purée	A soup that is thickened with the puréed vegetables with which it is made and flavoured.	5 mm croûtons served separately
Cream	A creamy soup that is finished with cream and is: • a purée base with milk; • a purée base with béchamel; • a velouté base with cream.	The garnish is dependent upon the type of soup, e.g. a cauliflower sprig for cream of cauliflower

There are many convenience soup products available. Most of them are of an acceptable standard, but few of them are as good as a soup that has been freshly made.

Sauces

A sauce is a liquid which has been thickened by any of the following agents:
- A roux — equal quantities of fat and flour, cooked.
- Cornflour — blended to a paste with liquid.
- Arrowroot — blended to a paste with liquid.
- Beurre manié — pellets of fat and flour, blended together.
- Egg yolks — beaten.

All sauces should be smooth, glossy in appearance, and adequately seasoned.

The purpose of sauces:
- To give flavour to dull insipid foods;
- To add nutritive value to foods;
- To counteract the richness of foods;
- To improve the appearance of foods;
- To give additional texture to foods;
- To add colour to foods;
- To bind foods together.

The aims of saucemaking:
- Careful blending of ingredients,
- Adequate seasoning to complement the sauce;
- Suitability of the sauce for the food;
- Preservation of a definite flavour and colour.

The standard proportions for basic sauces are as follows:

Pouring consistency	• Used for sauce that is to be served from a sauce-boat to accompany a dish.	• 15–20 g fat 15–20 g flour 250 ml liquid
Coating consistency	• Used to coat a food before it is to be served to the customer	• 25 g fat 25 g flour 250 ml liquid
Panada consistency	• Used to bind two or more foods together.	• 50 g fat 50 g flour 250 ml liquid

Method of Preparation

1. Melt fat in a thick-based saucepan.
2. Add the flour and mix in well with a wooden spoon.
3. Cook for a few minutes over a gentle heat:
    — without colouring for a white roux,
    — until of a sandy texture and colour for a blond roux,
    — until of a mid-brown colour for a brown roux.
4. Gradually add warmed liquid away from the heat, beat until smooth.
5. Return to the heat, stirring all the time until the sauce is boiling and smooth.
6. Allow the sauce to simmer gently for the required length of time:
    — 1 hour with clouté onion for a white roux;
    — 30 minutes for a blond roux;
    — 6 hours with browned chopped vegetables for a brown roux.
7. Pass the sauce through a fine strainer to correct the texture.
8. Re-heat the sauce then season to correct the flavour.

Faults in Sauce-making

Lumpiness	• Caused by the roux being too dry when the liquid is added • The liquid being added too quickly • Allowing a skin to form on the top while cooking • Allowing the sauce to become congealed on the sides of the pan
Poor gloss	• Insufficient cooking of the sauce • Sauce not strained properly
Incorrect consistency	• Too thick — excessive evaporation of the sauce allowed • Too thin — insufficient cooking at boiling point
Greasiness	• Incorrect balance in roux • Greasy liquid used and no skimming of the surface
Flavour	• Raw starch — insufficient cooking of starch • Bitter — brown roux over cooked

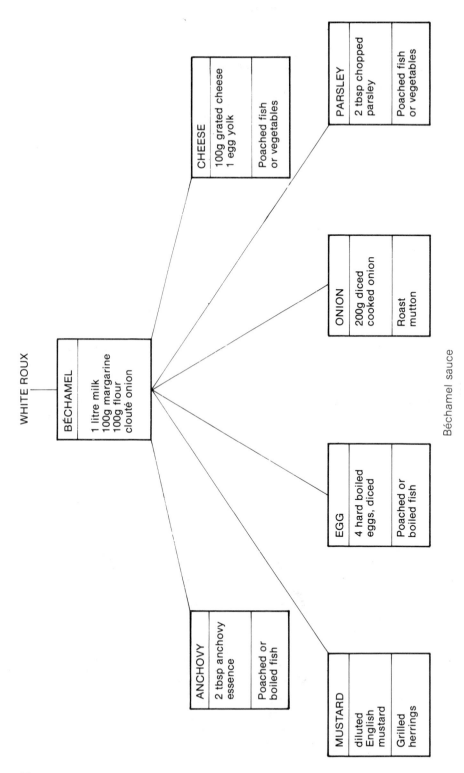

Béchamel sauce

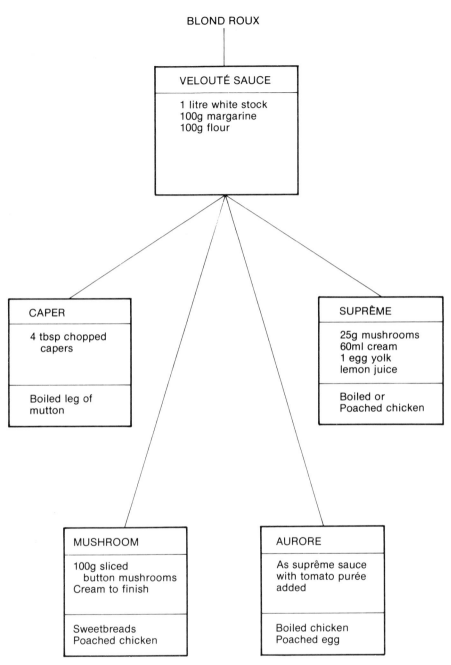

BLOND ROUX

VELOUTÉ SAUCE

1 litre white stock
100g margarine
100g flour

CAPER

4 tbsp chopped
  capers

Boiled leg of
mutton

SUPRÊME

25g mushrooms
60ml cream
1 egg yolk
lemon juice

Boiled or
Poached chicken

MUSHROOM

100g sliced
  button mushrooms
Cream to finish

Sweetbreads
Poached chicken

AURORE

As suprême sauce
with tomato purée
added

Boiled chicken
Poached egg

Note: The type of stock may be changed to complement the accompanying dish for the sauce, i.e.
- chicken stock for chicken dishes,
- veal stock for veal dishes,
- mutton stock for mutton dishes,
- fish stock for fish dishes.

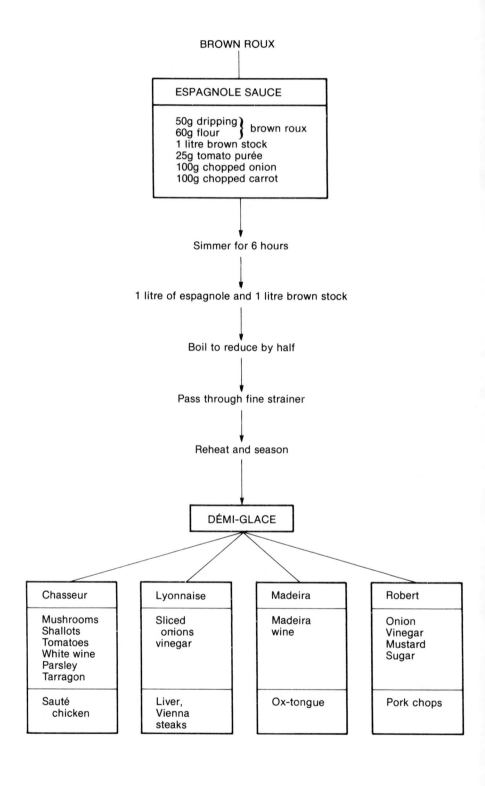

BROWN ROUX

ESPAGNOLE SAUCE

50g dripping ⎱ brown roux
60g flour ⎰
1 litre brown stock
25g tomato purée
100g chopped onion
100g chopped carrot

Simmer for 6 hours

1 litre of espagnole and 1 litre brown stock

Boil to reduce by half

Pass through fine strainer

Reheat and season

DÉMI-GLACE

Chasseur	Lyonnaise	Madeira	Robert
Mushrooms Shallots Tomatoes White wine Parsley Tarragon	Sliced onions vinegar	Madeira wine	Onion Vinegar Mustard Sugar
Sauté chicken	Liver, Vienna steaks	Ox-tongue	Pork chops

Other Sauces

Sauce	Ingredients	Served with
Tomato	Mirepoix of vegetables, tomato purée, blond roux, white stock	Spaghetti, eggs, meats, fish in batter
Bread	Milk, clouté onion (see p. 56), white breadcrumbs, butter	Roast chicken, roast game
Cranberry	Cranberries, sugar, water	Roast turkey
Apple	Bramley apples, sugar, pepper, butter	Roast pork, roast duck, roast game
Thickened gravy	Root vegetables, tomato purée, cornflour, brown stock	Meat dishes, rechauffé meat dishes (see pages 130 and 132)
Roast gravy	Onion, carrot, celery, brown stock, meat juices	Roast joints of meat
Mint	Chopped mint leaves, sugar, vinegar	Roast joints of lamb

Convenience sauces

There are many types of convenience sauce-mixes available to the caterer; some are of a very acceptable standard, while others are not as useful. They fall into three main categories:

Canned
- A condensed sauce, to be diluted by half and used with any fresh commodity
- Wine sauce
  Mushroom sauce
  Tomato sauce

Dehydrated
- A powder to be mixed with water, boiled and then simmered for 5 or 10 minutes
- Chasseur sauce
  Apple sauce
  Thickened gravy

Instant
- Granules, add boiling water, ready to use instantly
- Parsley sauce
  Cheese sauce
  Thickened gravy

Farinaceous Foods

Farinaceous means starchy; it is the term used to describe pasta and cereal products that contain a high level of starch. Italian pastes — or pasta — were originally made and cooked immediately as required, and were therefore not the dried pastas that are now available to the caterer. These dried pastas are produced in many countries for home consumption and for export; they are made from white or wholemeal flour and constitute a considerable part of the average diet in some countries.

Basic pasta is made from durum wheat flour, salt, water, fat or oil, and sometimes also egg. The nutritional value of pasta will depend upon the type of flour used and upon whether egg is used in the basic pasta recipe. Durum wheat flour is used because the gluten content is higher and this enables the pasta to retain its shape.

Method of cooking pasta

Pasta should be placed in a large pan of boiling salted water and then boiled gently until it is just softened right through. Sufficient boiling water must be used to enable the pasta to move and float about in the pan during cooking, to prevent it from becoming a starchy mass. Over-cooking the pasta will make its subsequent use limited, as the starch in the pasta will become slimy and cause the pieces to stick together. When softened, the cooked pasta must be immediately drained and rinsed under running water to wash away the excess starch. This rinsing will ensure that each piece of pasta will remain separate when used in the final dish.

If the pasta is to be served as an accompaniment, such as buttered noodles, it is tossed in melted butter over medium heat, which ensures that the pasta is reheated effectively after being rinsed. It is then sprinkled with freshly ground pepper and served immediately.

Pasta is usually served in shallow earthenware dishes, placed on a dish paper and silver flat.

The advantages of pasta

- Low price
- Long shelf-life
- Easily obtainable
- Short cooking time
- Compact storage
- Versatile uses
- Variety of types available
- Sustaining food — high starch content
- Good nutritional value
- Acceptable in fast-food and other outlets

Examples of Pasta

Type	Shape	Uses
Spaghetti	Fine tube shape	Spaghetti Bolognaise Spaghetti Napolitaine
Macaroni	Wide tube shape	Macaroni au Gratin
Noodles	Flat ribbon shape	Noodles in butter
Ravioli	Pasta envelopes filled with meat	Served with tomato sauce or demi-glace sauce
Cannelloni	Rolls of pasta with a meat filling	Baked in oven with cheese or tomato sauce
Lasagne	Wide pasta strips	Layered in a dish with meat and cheese sauces and baked in oven

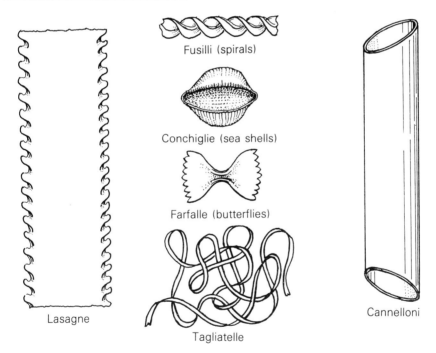

Fusilli (spirals)

Conchiglie (sea shells)

Farfalle (butterflies)

Lasagne

Tagliatelle

Cannelloni

Types of pasta

Cereals

Cereals are the seed grains of cultivated grasses — oats, wheat, barley, and rice. Some grains included in the cereal category are in fact obtained from the crushed roots or tubers of plants, e.g.

sago, tapioca, and arrowroot. Cereals are very versatile and easily obtained. They are used in a variety of ways, their main properties being their ability to thicken a liquid and their baking potential when ground to a flour.

Storage
Unopened sacks of grain or flour should be kept on racks well above floor level, in a well-ventilated dry storeroom. They should be used in rotation, using the oldest stock first, and regular checks for pest damage should be made.

In working kitchen areas cereals should be stored in airtight containers, or bins on wheels, to keep the cereals and flours free from moisture and contamination.

Types of Cereals

Cereal	Composition	Food value	Uses
Semolina	Crushed endosperm of wheat. Creamy granules	Starch	Milk puddings
Cornflour	Fine white powder from crushed corn	Starch	Thickened sauces Sweet moulds
Oats, rolled Oatmeal	Crushed oats Ground oats	Protein, fat, iron, calcium vitamin B	Porridge Flapjacks Biscuits Coating foods
Pearl barley Barley flour	Rounded polished grain Fine white powder	Starch	Soups, broths Barley water
Arrowroot	Fine white powder	Starch	Fruit glazes
Tapioca	Seeds or flakes	Starch	Milk puddings
Sago	Small white pellets	Starch	Milk puddings
Rice, Patna	Narrow pointed grain	Starch	Boiled rice
Carolina	Short round grain	Starch	Milk puddings
medium	Medium-sized grain	Starch	Risotto pilaff
ground	White fine grain	Starch	Milk puddings
brown	Grain with outer skin	Vitamin B	Braised or boiled
Rice flour	Fine grain	Starch	Thickening soups
Rice paper	Thin edible paper	Cellulose	Baking, sweets

Nutritional Qualities of Rice

Although the protein content of the rice is extremely low, the amino acids present in rice are a valuable complement to other foods that it may accompany, such as rice and chicken or fish, i.e. the combined nutritive value of the amino acids in the rice and other food is greater than would be obtained if the two foods were eaten separately.

Rice may be used in low-protein and low-fat diets. It needs only a small storage area and has a long shelf-life. It is easily obtainable and needs no preparation prior to cooking.

Rice and Pasta Dishes

Boiled rice
Use one volume of Patna rice to two volumes of liquid. The rice is placed in a pan with the liquid, brought to the boil, stirred once, and left with a well fitting lid at just below boiling point until the liquid is all absorbed and the rice is soft, but not all in a lump.

Braised Rice Pilaff
Long grain rice is cooked in white stock in a hot oven until all the stock has been absorbed. Diced cooked meat, fish and mixed vegetables may be forked into the rice to increase the flavour.

Risotto
Short grain rice is cooked gently in a sauteuse in white stock until all the stock is absorbed and the rice is soft. Diced cooked meats, fish, and vegetables may be forked into the rice before it is served.

Spaghetti Italienne
Cooked spaghetti is tossed in melted butter, grated cheese and black pepper. It is served in a shallow earthenware dish, placed on a silver flat, with grated Parmesan cheese served separately.

Macaroni au Gratin
Macaroni is cooked and coated in a well seasoned mornay sauce, placed in a shallow earthenware dish, gratinated under a grill, and placed on a silver flat dish for service.

Spaghetti Napolitaine
Cooked spaghetti is coated in well seasoned tomato sauce and tomato concassé, placed in a shallow earthenware dish on a silver flat and served with grated Parmesan cheese offered separately.

Spaghetti Milanaise
Cooked spaghetti is coated in well seasoned tomato sauce with julienne of ham, tongue and mushrooms, mixed in. It is served in a shallow earthenware dish on a silver flat, with grated Parmesan cheese served separately.

Spaghetti Bolognaise
Cooked spaghetti is tossed in melted butter, placed on a shallow

dish and a well seasoned meat sauce is poured over the centre. Grated Parmesan cheese is offered separately.

Ravioli

The filled pasta is poached then drained and coated in a rich tomato or demi-glace sauce. It is gratinated in a shallow dish and placed on a silver flat dish for service.

Pulses

These are the dried seeds of plants which form pods. They are useful as inexpensive contributors of vegetable protein and carbohydrate to the diet, especially in vegetarian dishes. Before being used by the caterer they must be soaked in cold water for twenty-four hours.

Type	Characteristics	Uses
Butter beans	Oval, off white colour	Soup, vegetable dishes
Haricot beans	Small oval, off white	Soup, haricot mutton
Green peas	Whole or split, dull green	Soup, vegetable dishes
Yellow peas	Whole or split, dull yellow	Soup, pease pudding
Lentils	Orange-red colour, split	Soup, stews, cutlets or burgers
Soya beans	Oval, off white colour, high in protein	Textured vegetable protein, flour

Vegetarian food

There are two types of vegetarians: strict vegetarians, or vegans, who for personal or religious reasons will not eat any animal flesh of any kind, nor eggs, milk, cheese or animal products. This diet is very limited and care has to be taken when balancing the protein content of this type of diet. Secondly, there are lacto-vegetarians, (or lacto-ovo-vegetarians), who will not eat any animal flesh but will eat cheese, milk and often eggs. This type of diet is relatively easy to plan and balance as the protein intake is supplied by the cheese, milk, and eggs.

When planning a vegan diet the following considerations, with regard to nutritional balance, must be taken into account:

- Protein will be obtained from pulses, soya bean products, lentils, nuts of all types, and cereals.
- Vitamin A found in margarine, vegetables, dried apricots and prunes.

50

- Vitamin B will be supplied in yeast extract, oatmeal, whole grains, nuts, pulses and vegetables.
- Vitamin C found in fresh fruits and raw vegetables.
- Vitamin D will be supplied in margarine and manufactured by the skin when subjected to sunlight.
- Minerals, such as calcium, phosphorus and iron, will be supplied by green vegetables, such as watercress, cabbage, spinach, kale, and by nuts.

Vegetables

Group	Properties	Examples	Quality
Roots	Variety of colour, texture, and flavour. Versatile	Carrots, parsnips, beetroot, swedes, turnips	No spade marks, insect bites, or excess soil. Even shape
Tubers	Provide vitamin C, carbohydrate, and bulk to a meal	Potatoes, Jerusalem artichokes	No sign of green flesh, firm, no insect bites, no excess soil
Bulbs	Definite flavour used to enhance flavour of foods	Onions, shallots, leeks, garlic	Firm flesh, smooth glossy skins, no bruising or dampness
Leaves	Provide vitamin C, iron, roughage. Add colour and texture to meal	Cabbage, lettuce, spinach, Brussels sprouts, spring greens	Crisp green leaves. No sign of browning or yellow and no slugs or caterpillars on leaves
Flowers	Add variety of shape and texture. Delicate flavour	Cauliflower, globe artichokes, broccoli	Undamaged heads, close, crisp flowers, no flies or brown bruising marks
Fruits	Good variety of flavours, shapes, colours and textures	Tomatoes, marrows, courgettes, cucumbers, peppers	Unbroken skin, firm flesh, good even colour, no bruising or fly infestation
Legumes	Provide vegetable protein. Variety of colour and shape	Peas, broad beans, runner beans	Firm full shells, no insect bites or bruising
Blanched stem	Crisp texture, delicate flavour	Celery, chicory, asparagus	Clean crisp stems. No bruising or slug bites
Fungi	Definite flavour, dark colouring	Mushrooms — flat, and button	Firm dry flesh, no sign of stickiness or mould

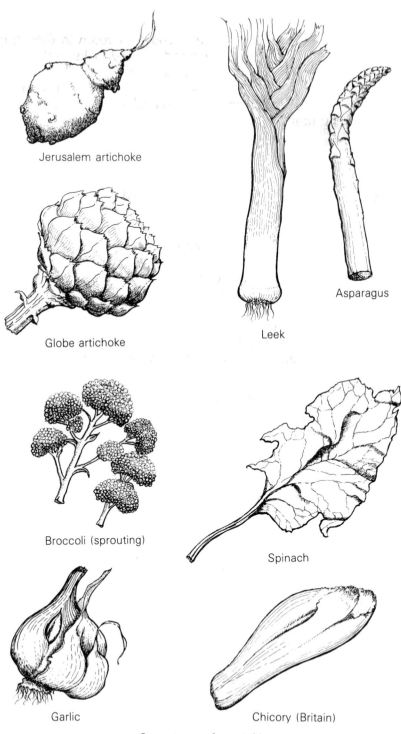

Jerusalem artichoke

Globe artichoke

Leek

Asparagus

Broccoli (sprouting)

Spinach

Garlic

Chicory (Britain)

Some types of vegetables

Storage of Vegetables

All vegetables should be stored in a cool airy room in their trays, crates, or sacks, placed on well-spaced, slatted racks, out of direct sunlight and lightly covered to keep as clean as possible. Leaves, flowers, fruits, blanched stems, legumes and fungi all have a short shelf life and should therefore be purchased as required, not stored in the catering unit.

The Cooking and Serving of Vegetables

Methods used

- *Boiled* — tubers, roots, leaves, flowers, pulses.
- *Roast* — potatoes, parsnips.
- *Braised* — onions, celery, cabbage.
- *Sauté* — potatoes, mushrooms, onions, parsnips.
- *Steamed* — tubers, roots, flowers.
- *Deep fried* — potatoes, onions, mushrooms.
- *Grilled* — tomatoes, mushrooms, potato dishes.
- *Microwave* — small quantities of frozen vegetables.

Roasting
- Prepare the vegetables and par-boil or brown quickly on top of the range.
- Place the vegetables in melted fat in a roasting tin, sprinkled with salt. Cook in a hot oven until soft inside and crisp brown outside. Drain off any excess fat.

Braising
- Prepare the vegetables. Place a little fat in the base of a casserole with a well fitting lid, place a layer of rough cut root vegetables in the casserole, sprinkle with salt and pepper.
- Place the whole vegetables to be braised on top of this. Cover with the lid and cook for 10 minutes. Then add sufficient stock just to cover the base vegetables only. Replace the lid.
- Cook in a moderate oven until the whole vegetables are tender.

Sautéing
- For root vegetables: prepare the vegetables and par-boil for five minutes, then toss in hot fat in a sauté pan. Season well with salt and pepper. They should be lightly coloured.
- For potatoes: the potatoes are boiled or steamed in their skins, and peeled while still hot. They are sliced to 1cm thick and tossed in hot fat until golden brown, then drained well and served sprinkled with salt and chopped parsley.

Steaming
- Prepare the vegetables and place on steamer trays/racks, sprinkled with salt.
- Cook in the steamer for 30–60 minutes, depending upon the size and type of the vegetable.

Baking
- The potatoes are scrubbed clean and then pricked all over with a fine skewer. They are then placed on a baking sheet and sprinkled with salt.
- They are cooked in a moderate oven until the potatoes are soft inside. They are served with a slit in the top filled with a knob of chilled butter.

Aims when cooking
- To soften the fibres and minimise the absorption of water.
- To make the starch content more digestible.
- To preserve the natural colour, texture and flavour.
- To cook with the minimum loss of nutrients.

Reasons for cooking
- Many vegetables are difficult to digest when raw.
- The cellulose is softened and their bulk is reduced.

How to preserve the nutritive value
- Use vegetables when fresh and peel as thinly as possible, using a sharp knife to prevent cell damage.
- Prepare as close to the cooking time as is possible.
- Never soak or leave in water as the soluble vitamins will be lost.
- Always cook vegetables in the minimum amount of water to prevent loss of vitamins.
- If the vegetables have to be kept hot, they should be only just tender, as the heat in the bain-marie will continue to cook them.

Service
- Always use hot dishes with lids, unless the vegetables have been fried or roasted or sautéed.
- Serve as soon as possible after cooking.
- Always cook for the minimum time possible.
- Boiled vegetables may be brushed with, or tossed in, melted butter prior to service to give an extra richness of flavour and a glossy appearance.

- Some vegetables can be successfully braised, either whole or with a stuffing, these are then served with a sauce made from the braising liquor.
- Some vegetables may be cooked and then served coated in a complementary sauce, e.g. cauliflower and a mornay sauce, broad beans and a parsley sauce, beetroot and a cream sauce.

Convenience vegetables

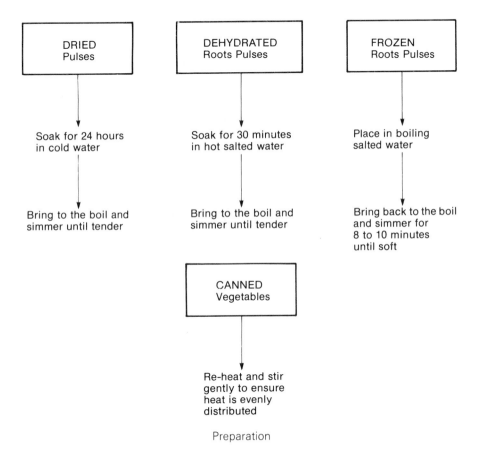

Preparation

Advantages

- They can be used to supplement fresh items.
- They add variety of colour and shape.
- Dried pulses increase nutritional value of foods.
- Frozen and canned are quick to use.
- Dehydrated and dried items need a small storage area.

Vegetable Terms and Cuts

Duxelle
Finely chopped shallots and mushrooms, sweated in butter until they are soft and the moisture has evaporated. Seasoned and finished with chopped parsley. Used for stuffing vegetables.

Tomato concassé
Whole firm tomatoes are peeled, then quartered and the pips removed. The remaining tomato flesh is coarsely chopped and often sweated with chopped shallots. Used for items such as marquise potatoes and in some sauces.

Clouté onion
Small peeled onion that is studded with cloves, then used to flavour liquids by infusion. Used in the flavouring of béchamel sauce.

Mirepoix
Diced prepared carrots, celery, and onion, with parsley and thyme; used as the base for an item to be braised.

Diced
Vegetables cut to even-sized cubes.

Rough chopped
Vegetables chopped to small pieces, used in soup and sauce-making.

Bouquetière
Mixture of prepared vegetables served together on one dish, each vegetable should be of a different shape and colour.

Macédoine
A mixture of vegetables creating a good contrast of colour and flavour. Diced to 5mm size and, when cooked, tossed together prior to service. Often used as a vegetable accompaniment to a meat dish.

Tourne vegetables
Tuber or root vegetables are turned with a small knife to create eight-sided barrel shapes, 3cm in length. These are used for garnishing ragoûts or similar dishes. This is also used to produce pommes fondantes and pommes château.

Standard vegetable cuts

Julienne Cut to 3cm × 2.5mm thin strips

Brunoise Cut to 2mm dice

Macédoine Cut to 5mm dice

Jardinère Cut to batons 2 × 2 × 15mm

Paysanne • Cut flat to 1cm triangles
• Cut flat to 1cm squares
• Cut flat to 1cm circles
• Cut flat to 1cm edged rounds

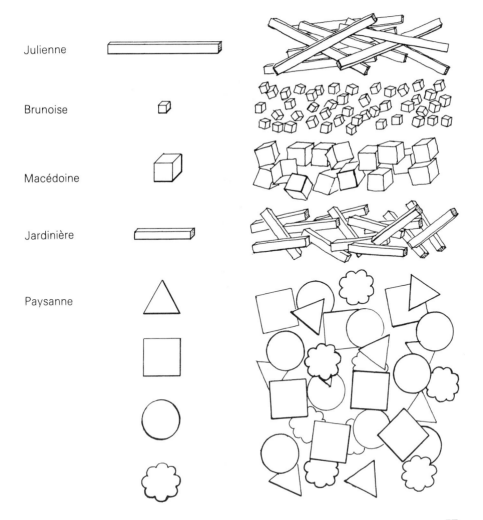

Julienne

Brunoise

Macédoine

Jardinière

Paysanne

Potatoes

The ways of serving potatoes are numerous, but the real test of skill in potato cookery is the ability to cook them to perfection using simple methods.

For boiling, steaming, roasting or deep frying, old potatoes are the most satisfactory; but when shallow frying potatoes, or making potato salad, new potatoes will give a better result. Younger potatoes are richer in protein than the older ones, and are solid, waxy and juicy in texture when cooked. As the starch cells are immature in new potatoes, they are not as easily digested as old potatoes.

The main nutrients found in potatoes are: starch, water, vitamin C, and cellulose.

Varieties of potato

Majestic
• Main crop potato with a white skin and firm texture
• Suitable for frying
Arran Pilot
• Early variety potato, good sized
• Suitable for boiling and baking
Epicure
• Early variety potato with a pink skin and white flesh
• Suitable for boiling and baking
King Edward
• Main crop potato, slightly pink skin and creamy white flesh
• Suitable for most methods of cooking
Golden Wonder
• Popular main crop potato, pale brown skin and creamy white close textured flesh
• Suitable for all types of fried dishes and roasting

Convenience potato products

As potatoes are so versatile and easily obtained, there are many convenience potato products available:
Canned
• New potatoes in salted water, ready for instant use.
• Potato salad in mayonnaise, ready for instant use.
Frozen
• Blanched — roast and chipped potatoes that may be deep fried or oven-baked from frozen.
• Prepared — croquettes and balls in batter, may be deep fried or oven-baked from frozen.

Dehydrated
- Instant potato flakes or powder may be reconstituted with boiling water, butter and seasonings.

Packet crisps/sticks
- Various flavours and shapes are available. The packets are in 28 g size for individual portions or larger packets for bulk uses. These products have a short shelf life of 3 months maximum.

Examples of potato dishes

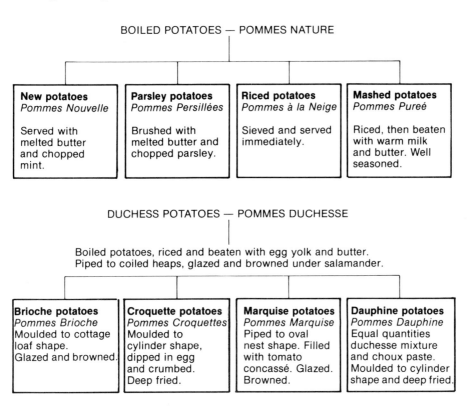

BOILED POTATOES — POMMES NATURE

New potatoes *Pommes Nouvelle* Served with melted butter and chopped mint.	**Parsley potatoes** *Pommes Persillées* Brushed with melted butter and chopped parsley.	**Riced potatoes** *Pommes à la Neige* Sieved and served immediately.	**Mashed potatoes** *Pommes Pureé* Riced, then beaten with warm milk and butter. Well seasoned.

DUCHESS POTATOES — POMMES DUCHESSE

Boiled potatoes, riced and beaten with egg yolk and butter.
Piped to coiled heaps, glazed and browned under salamander.

Brioche potatoes *Pommes Brioche* Moulded to cottage loaf shape. Glazed and browned.	**Croquette potatoes** *Pommes Croquettes* Moulded to cylinder shape, dipped in egg and crumbed. Deep fried.	**Marquise potatoes** *Pommes Marquise* Piped to oval nest shape. Filled with tomato concassé. Glazed. Browned.	**Dauphine potatoes** *Pommes Dauphine* Equal quantities duchesse mixture and choux paste. Moulded to cylinder shape and deep fried.

STEAMED POTATOES — POMMES VAPOUR

Jacket potatoes
Pommes en Robe de Chambre

Even-sized potatoes,
scrubbed and cooked
in steamer. Served
unpeeled with the
top slit open and a
knob of butter inserted.

Shallow-fried potatoes
Pommes Sautées

Potatoes steamed in
their skins then
peeled and sliced.
Tossed in hot fat until
golden brown.

Fried potatoes and onion
Pommes Lyonnaise

Sauté potatoes
combined with fried
onion rings. Served
with chopped parsley
and ground salt.

POTATOES BAKED IN SKINS — POMMES AU FOUR

Baked in jackets with cheese
Pommes Gratinées

Halved baked potatoes mixed with
cheese, re-filled and gratinated.

Macaire potatoes
Pommes Macaire

Potatoes scooped out and mixed with
milk and butter. Moulded to flat
cakes, floured and shallow fried.

POTATOES COOKED WITH STOCK

Savoury potatoes
Pommes Boulangère

Thin slices of potato and onion,
layered in earthenware dish,
just covered with white stock.
Seasoned and baked in oven.

Fondant potatoes
Pommes Fondant

Potatoes turned to eight-sided barrel shapes.
Brushed with melted butter and cooked in tin
half-covered with white stock. Basted and
baked to golden brown.

ROAST POTATOES — POMMES ROTIES

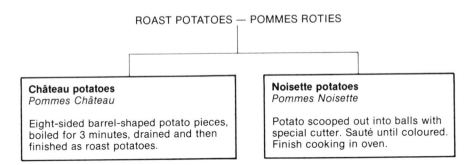

Château potatoes
Pommes Château

Eight-sided barrel-shaped potato pieces, boiled for 3 minutes, drained and then finished as roast potatoes.

Noisette potatoes
Pommes Noisette

Potato scooped out into balls with special cutter. Sauté until coloured. Finish cooking in oven.

DEEP-FRIED

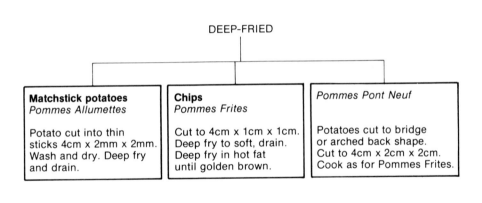

Matchstick potatoes
Pommes Allumettes

Potato cut into thin sticks 4cm x 2mm x 2mm. Wash and dry. Deep fry and drain.

Chips
Pommes Frites

Cut to 4cm x 1cm x 1cm. Deep fry to soft, drain. Deep fry in hot fat until golden brown.

Pommes Pont Neuf

Potatoes cut to bridge or arched back shape. Cut to 4cm x 2cm x 2cm. Cook as for Pommes Frites.

SHALLOW-FRIED

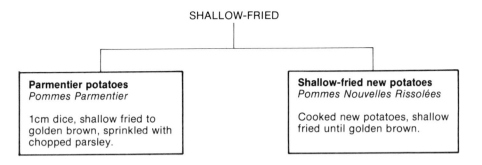

Parmentier potatoes
Pommes Parmentier

1cm dice, shallow fried to golden brown, sprinkled with chopped parsley.

Shallow-fried new potatoes
Pommes Nouvelles Rissolées

Cooked new potatoes, shallow fried until golden brown.

Unit 3 Assessment Activities

1. (a) Prepare a brown beef stock and compare this with various types of convenience stock products.
   (b) Analyse the results in terms of the preparation time, cost, and flavour.

2. (a) Prepare a béchamel sauce and then make some of the sauces derivative from this.
   (b) Taste and compare the sauces made with regard to colour, flavour, and texture.
   (c) List some suitable uses for each of the sauces that have been made.

3. (a) Make a collection of types of pasta, rice, and cereals that are available in your area.
   (b) Mount the samples on card and create a display.
   (c) Make a chart to illustrate the nutritional values of these products.
   (d) List suitable recipes that illustrate the use of pasta, rice, and cereals.

4. (a) Visit your local greengrocer and list the types and cost of the vegetables that are for sale.
   (b) Describe how to prepare and cook and serve 4 of the more unusual vegetables that you have seen.

5. (a) Prepare two or three potato dishes from the same basic method.
   (b) Invite colleagues to taste these samples and to indicate their preferences.
   (c) Analyse these preferences in terms of cost, taste, and appearance.

Unit 4:

Fruits and Pastry Work

Fruits

Fresh fruits should be used when they are just ripe. Under-ripe fruit may be difficult to digest, especially if eaten raw, because of excess fruit acids. Over-ripe fruit may contain bacteria which will upset the digestion.

There is a large amount of water in fruit — up to 85 per cent — which gives the fruit its refreshing quality. Fruit is eaten raw for the vitamin C content, roughage in the form of cellulose, and its flavour. Raw fruit contains more vitamin C than cooked. Fruits contain a good supply of fruit acids, the supply of which increases as the fruit ripens. Acids help the laxative action of fruit by stimulating the action of the intestines. The fruit acids help in the setting of jams with pectin.

There are numerous tropical fruits that are now becoming increasingly popular when eaten in their fresh state. They are used to supplement the more usual varieties of fruits that are available. These less common fruits are imported and sold as and when they are in season, thus increasing the variety of fruits that are available to the caterer.

Classification of Fruits

Group	Fruit	Convenience products	Quality points — Fresh fruits
Soft	Strawberries Raspberries Blackcurrants Gooseberries	Canned in syrup Frozen Jams. Cordials Canned pie fillings	Firm, good colour. No bruises or insect bites. Minimum number of stalks or leaves.
Hard	Cooking apples Dessert apples Pears	Canned in syrup or solid pack. Frozen. Dehydrated flakes. Dried.	Crisp with good colour. No bruising or insect bites. Thin clear skins and short stalks.
Stone	Plums Peaches Cherries	Canned in syrup or solid pack. Jams. Pie fillings. Glacé. Dried.	Good clear colour. No wasp bites or bruises, no broken skin. No leaves or long stalks.
Citrus	Oranges Grapefruit Lemons Mandarins Tangerines	Juices. Canned in own juice. Marmalade. Candied peel. Cordials. Slices bottled for drinks. Frozen.	No green areas on the skin, firm even skin, no lumps. No brown patches or soft areas.
Tropical	Pineapple Melon Bananas	Canned in syrup. Juices, frozen. Candied. Dehydrated.	Good colour, firm. No blemishes.

Uses

Fruits may be used in many different ways and parts of a menu; for example they are frequently used in hors d'oeuvres or fruit cocktails and juices. They may be used to garnish foods, such as poultry and fish dishes, and fruits are also made into sauces to accompany meat and poultry, their tartness complementing the richness of the meat. In sweet desserts fruits are used in hot and cold pastry and sponge-based dishes. Their versatility and variety of colour, flavour and texture makes them invaluable.

Cooking increases the digestibility of soft, stone and hard fruits by softening the fibres and destroying any bacteria present in the fresh commodity. But most of the vitamin C content of fruit is destroyed by cooking; it is also lost when fruit is peeled and prepared for further use and by prolonged storage.

Cooking of Fresh Fruits

Poaching	• Soft fruits:	Hot syrup is gently poured over the prepared fruit.
	• Other fruit:	Prepared fruit is gently poached in syrup until it is just soft, but not broken up in any way.
Baking	• Apples:	The core is hollowed out and the centre filled with Demerara sugar and/or dried fruit. 50ml of water is added. The apples are baked in a moderate oven until soft but still in shape.
Steaming	• Apples, rhubarb, pears:	They are prepared and placed in shallow trays with a small amount of water. The trays are covered and placed in the steamer. They are cooked until the fruit is softened but not broken up in any way. This method is useful when preparing fruit pies and puddings, as the steaming does not dilute the flavour; the steamed fruit may be sweetened as required when the pies are prepared.
Deep frying	• Pineapple, apples, bananas:	Prepared and floured, then dipped into a yeast batter and fried until the batter is a golden brown and crisp.

Puddings containing a high proportion of fruit

- Pies and tartlets *using:* apples, blackberry and apple, gooseberries, rhubarb, damsons, plums, cherries, blackcurrants.
- Suet puddings *using:* apples, blackberry and apple, plums, dates, currants.

- Sponge puddings *using:* apples, pineapples, raspberries, blackcurrants, sultanas.
- Flans *using:* apples, bananas, strawberries, raspberries, peaches, pears.

Preservation of Fruits

Method	Fruits	Uses
Dehydrated	Apple rings, figs, dates, currants, sultanas, raisins, apricot halves, peach halves, pear halves, prunes, bananas.	Dried fruit salad. Stewed fruits. Steamed fruit puddings and dumplings. Fruit cakes. Mince pies.
Canned	Solid packed apples, damsons and rhubarb. Mandarins, grapefruit, cherries, gooseberries, peaches, plums, mixed fruits.	Fruit pies, crumbles, tarts. Fruit gâteaux. Fruit salads. Sweet pastry flans and tarts. Puff pastry fruit items.
Candied	Oranges, limes, lemons, grapefruit.	Fruit cakes. Eccles cakes. Mince pies. Christmas pudding.
Crystallized	Peaches, oranges, lemons, plums, greengages, cherries, mandarins	Whole fruits served in the dessert fruit course of the meal.
Glacé	Cherries.	Cakes. Decorating bakery items.
Frozen	Apples, gooseberries, rhubarb, plums, blackcurrants, melon, blackberries, raspberries, mixed fruits.	Fruit puddings and sponges. Fruit crumbles. Pastry flans and puff pastry items. Fruit salads and cocktails.
Juices	Oranges, grapefruits, tomatoes, pineapples, apples, blackcurrants, mixed tropical fruits, mixed citrus fruits.	Chilled as an appetizer. With an alcoholic drink as a mixer. Fruit punches and cocktails.
Jam	Raspberries, blackcurrants, strawberries, blackberry and apple, plums, damsons, apricots, mixed fruits, citrus fruits as marmalade.	Served to accompany toast, scones, or tea cakes. Used in baked products to glaze, or fill pastry and cake items. Steamed puddings.

Nuts

Nuts are the edible seeds produced from a tree or plant. Generally nuts are not eaten in very large quantities although, with the increase of vegetarian and wholefood natural diets, their consumption is on the increase. This is mainly due to their nutritional content and versatility. Nuts contain a high percentage of carbohydrate in the form of starch, fat in the form of oils, and also protein, which makes them invaluable to vegetarians.

Nuts are added to breakfast cereals and are therefore consumed daily by numerous persons who would otherwise probably not benefit from their vegetable protein content.

Some nuts are dry roasted and tossed in seasonings and salt and then sealed in small foil sachets and retailed for snacks and to accompany alcoholic drinks. Peanuts are salted and then sold in sealed containers as accompaniments for drinks. Other mixed selections of prepared nuts are sold in packets with raisins, or used in many different types of snack biscuits and chocolate-based bars of confectionery. By these various retailing methods a large amount of nuts is consumed.

Prepared nuts

For kitchen use the following types of prepared nuts are available:

- *Ground* — almonds, hazelnuts *for* frangipane, marzipan, meringue-based items.
- *Nibbed* — almonds, peanuts *for* decorating iced dishes, pastry goods.
- *Flaked* — almonds *for* decorating cakes and pastries.
- *Halved* — almonds, walnuts *for* salads, in cakes, decorating cakes.
- *Whole* — almonds, hazelnuts *for* decorating cakes and pastries.
- *Desiccated* — coconut *for* flavouring cakes, decorating cakes, curries.
- *Essence* — almond *for* flavouring cakes and fillings.

Note: All these prepared nuts should be kept in airtight containers in a cool, dry store room.

Fresh nuts

Whole dessert nuts are available in their shells during the late autumn and early winter months. They are retailed in their fresh state and should therefore be selected to ensure good quality. The shells should be unbroken, even-sized, with no sign of dampness or mould.

To store, they should be kept in a dry, well ventilated area with careful stock rotation, as they have a limited shelf life.

Sugar

Sugar beet

This is grown in the United Kingdom. The juice is extracted from the beet by shredding and heating. Impurities are then removed and the liquid crystallized to produce various grades of white sugar.

Sugar cane

This is grown in the Tropics and South America. The cane is crushed and the juice extracted. The juice is then boiled, the impurities removed and the syrup processed to produce various grades of brown then white types of sugar.

Sugar

Type	Characteristics	Uses
Caster	Fine white crystals	Bakery work, sugar sifters
Granulated	Crystals of medium size	General sweetening use
Cube/loaf	Crystals compressed to cubes	Afternoon tea service
Icing	Fine white powder	Cake icings
Preserving	Grains, to prevent a scum forming	Preserve making
Demerara	Golden brown crystals	Coffee service, some cooking
Barbados, dark	Moist fine grade, dark colour	Dark cakes and puddings
Barbados, light	Fine grade, light sandy colour	Light fruit cakes, biscuits
Coffee crystals	Irregular light brown crystals	Sweetening after dinner coffee
Golden syrup	Processed to a yellow syrup	Cooking and baking
Black treacle	Blended syrup and molasses	Cooking and confectionery
Molasses	Dark by-product of sugar	Cooking and confectionery

The effect of heat

Moist heat
Sugar dissolves more rapidly in hot water than in cold. Once heated it becomes a syrup. If heat is continuously applied to the syrup the water will begin to evaporate and the sugar will begin to turn a sandy colour; it will eventually caramelize and then burn to carbon.
Dry heat
The sugar will rapidly turn colour, caramelize and then burn, turning black.

	Degrees of cooking	Uses
Small thread	104°C	Stock syrups
Large thread	110°C	Crystallizing fruits
Soft ball	116°C	Fondant
Hard ball	121°C	Sweet-making
Small crack	140°C	Meringue
Large crack	153°C	Dipping individual fruits
Caramel	176°C	Crème caramel

Chocolate

Cocoa comes from the fruit of an evergreen tree which grows in America, the West Indies, South America, New Guinea and Central Africa. The seeds are roasted, cracked, and ground and the cocoa butter is then removed. The remaining cocoa is pressed together and then ground to a fine powder. Because of the high fat content, and the presence of carbohydrate and protein, cocoa is a nutritious commodity.

Cocoa is improved by boiling; it thickens slightly by cooking the starch content and holding the powder in suspension, thus producing a smooth liquid.

Cocoa products

Cocoa powder
• A fine brown powder which will go lumpy if allowed to come into contact with the atmosphere. It must therefore be stored in airtight containers in a cool dry place.

- It is used to make a hot cocoa beverage, and to flavour items in pastry work.
- It is necessary to blend the powder with a small quantity of liquid before incorporating it into any other commodity, as it will quickly form hard lumps when in contact with heat.

Drinking chocolate
- It is a light brown powder made by mixing cocoa powder, dried milk powder, sugar, vanilla and flavourings.
- It does not need to be boiled when preparing a hot beverage.
- It should be stored in airtight containers.
- It is used for making hot chocolate drinks, especially those sold from vending machines.
- It is used in a limited way in the bakery, for milk-chocolate flavoured butter icings and sponges.

Chocolate couverture
- It is a chocolate produced for confectionery work and may be melted and remoulded without any loss of gloss or colour.
- It has a low melting point and must therefore be melted slowly — too much heat will cause it to cook and thicken, making it unsuitable for further use.
- It is used in the bakery for coating and dipping small cakes and pastries.

Pastrywork Definitions

Apple charlotte: A pudding made from slices of bread and apple, baked in a mould, turned out to serve with an apricot sauce.
Apple flan: Sugar paste filled with apple, decorated with sliced apple and the flan glazed with apricot glaze.
Apricot glaze: Boiled apricot jam and a little water, strained and used hot.
Bakewell tart: Sugar paste base, frangipane filling spread on top of a thin layer of raspberry jam. Baked, then water iced.
Banana flan: Sugar paste base, filled with confectioner's custard and decorated with sliced bananas, glazed with apricot glaze.
Barquettes: Boat-shaped pastry tartlets, filled with a sweet or a savoury filling or just fresh fruits and glazed.
Bavarois: A cold sweet mould made from milk, cream, eggs, and gelatine; often flavoured and decorated.
Bun wash: Sugar and water boiled together to a thick syrup, used to glaze sweet dough goods.
Cabinet puddings: Pudding made from plain sponge, sultanas, cherries and a sweet custard base, baked in the oven in a dariole mould and turned out to serve, with apricot sauce.

70

Confectioner's custard: Made from milk, egg yolks, sugar, and flour, flavoured with vanilla essence. A thick creamy consistency.

Crème Chantilly: Whipped cream, sweetened with caster sugar and vanilla essence.

Crêpes: Very thin pancakes.

Dariole mould: A small mould (1 gill) used for puddings with sloping sides.

Diplomat pudding: This is a cabinet pudding that is baked in exactly the same way, then cooled in the mould and turned out when cold to be served. It may be decorated with cream.

Dutch apple tart: Sugar paste tart filled with apple and sultanas, flavoured with lemon juice and cinnamon.

Eccles cakes: Puff pastry circles, filled with dried fruit mix, spice and sugar, baked to a golden brown.

Fleurons: Crescent-shaped small pieces of puff paste used to garnish dishes.

Frangipane: A filling made from ground almonds, eggs, flour, sugar and butter.

Frappé: French word that means, 'to chill'.

Fruit pie: Fruit in pie dish with pastry on top.

Fruit slice: Puff paste rectangle case filled with fruit and glazed.

Fruit tart: Shallow dish with pastry top and bottom, fruit inside.

Fruit tartlet: Sugar paste, individual size, baked blind, filled with fruits.

Gâteau: A cake to be portioned for service, 8, 10 or 12 portions.

Genoese sponge: Whisked method of making a cake, with butter added. A base for many types of gâteau.

Gluten: This is the protein found in flour.

Jalousie: Puff paste rectangle filled with mincemeat, jam or frangipane, with a lattice top, baked and served in slices.

Junket: Slightly sweetened milk that is set with rennet. Sprinkled with grated nutmeg.

Meringue: Equal weights of egg white and caster sugar, whisked, piped and dried/set in a cool oven.

Palmiers: These are made from puff paste trimmings, rolled up and then sliced before baking in a hot oven. They are dredged in icing sugar before service.

Petits fours: Very small sweets and cakes. One mouthful size, served at the end of a meal with coffee and liqueurs.

Pithiviers: Puff paste circle, 25cm diameter, filled with frangipane and a lattice top placed on before baking.

Profiteroles: Small choux buns; may be filled with cream and served piled up in a dish with chocolate sauce poured over the top.

Proving: To allow a yeast mixture to rise and expand in a warm place.

Rum baba: Rich yeast dough with currrants, baked in dariole moulds, sprinkled with rum and apricot glaze.

Savarin: Rich yeast dough in ring mould, brushed with apricot glaze, filled with prepared fruits.

Soufflé: A light dish, sweet or savoury, made from eggs. It may be baked in the oven and served immediately, or set with gelatine and served when set and cold.

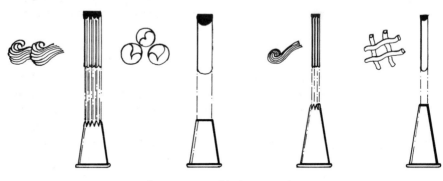

Some types of bakery nozzles

Terms used in pastry work

Beating: Care needs to be taken when beating cake mixtures, as over-beating can ruin the texture of a rich fuit cake, or sponge cake. However, it is essential when making gingerbread by the melting method. An electric mixer and beater attachment on medium speed may be used.

Consistency: This is the term given to the correct texture of the cake mixture before it is baked.

Soft dropping — the mixture will easily drop from the spoon or beater. A thick batter consistency.

Stiff dropping – the mixture will hold its shape when shaken from a spoon or beater, but is too soft and sticky to handle.

Soft dough — a soft mixture but not too soft to handle.

Creaming: Used for making many cakes. The fat should be at room temperature but not oily; the sugar and fat are then beaten together, either with a wooden spoon or with an electric mixer and a beater attachment at a medium speed. This beating is continued until the texture is light and fluffy, and a light cream colour. The remaining ingredients are then folded into this creamed mixture.

Folding in: It is a method of incorporating an ingredient into a mixture so as to preserve the maximum amount of air. The mixture in the bowl should be lightly stirred with a metal or plastic spoon in a short figure-of-eight movement, while giving the bowl a half turn with each fold. Lighter mixtures should be folded into heavier mixtures, such as whisked egg whites folded into a cake mixture, or sieved flour folded into a creamed mixture, so that the air is not pressed out.

Melting: Used when making gingerbreads and some biscuits. The fat, sugar, and syrup are gently heated until the fat has melted and the sugar has dissolved; the other ingredients are then beaten into these liquids. It results in a pouring consistency mixture, which requires baking at a slow to moderate temperature in a shallow tin to create a moist cake.

Rubbing in: Used for plain cakes, short pastry and biscuits. It is the process of incorporating the fat into the flour by rubbing it between the tips of the fingers, and lifting the mixture so that air is incorporated into the mixture. This is continued until the texture of fine breadcrumbs is obtained. This process may be achieved by an electric mixer by using a slow speed and a hook or beater attachment.

Whisking: This method is used for very light cakes. The air is incorporated by whisking eggs and caster sugar together until the mixture is light in colour and is thick enough to hold a 'trail'. An electric mixer and whisk attachment used at high speed is essential for successful results.

Egg whites — when just whisking egg whites, they must be separated carefully and whisked in a bowl that is free from any fat or grease. When a soft peak stage has been obtained, the whisked whites may be incorporated into the main cake mixture by a gentle folding method.

Wheat and Flour

Wheat is produced in the United Kingdom or imported from Canada. The Canadian wheat is the harder type and has a higher proportion of protein (gluten); this is used to produce the strong flour used in bread-making.

Flour is made from wheat by:

- Cleaning the grain of small seeds and dust by sieving.
- Passing the clean dry grain between rollers which crack and remove the outer layer.
- Returning the removed bran and aleurone layer to the rollers to remove the remaining endosperm particles.
- Crushing the endosperm to produce semolina.
- Rolling the semolina between smooth rollers to reduce it to a fine white powder — flour.

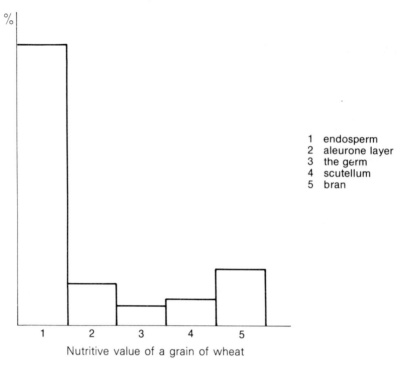

Nutritive value of a grain of wheat

1 endosperm
2 aleurone layer
3 the germ
4 scutellum
5 bran

- The *endosperm* consists of 85 per cent of the grain and contains carbohydrate and protein.
- The *aleurone layer* encloses the endosperm and is high in protein.
- The *germ* consists of 1.5 per cent of the grain and contains protein, fat and vitamin B.
- The *scutellum* encloses the germ and contains vitamin B (thiamine).
- The *bran*, or skin, consists of 13 per cent of the grain and contains cellulose, calcium, iron and phosphorus.

Types of flour

The milling process can be modified to give more or less flour from a given amount of wheat. The percentage of flour obtained is called the *extraction rate* of the flour. For example, true wholemeal flour has an extraction rate of 100 per cent, meaning that the whole grain has been converted into flour. It receives its brown colour from the pigment in the bran. As the extraction rate is lowered, the proportion of bran remaining in the flour decreases and so the colour becomes lighter and the flour more digestible, although less nutritious. Normally, white flour has an extraction rate of 70 per cent and contains only crushed endosperm — semolina.

In the United Kingdom, the nutritional value of flour is increased by the addition of the following nutrients — thiamine, nicotinic acid, and minerals in the form of iron and calcium. One hundred per cent wholemeal flour does not need any additional nutrients.

Ingredients for Pastry Work

Flour

- Plain soft flour is used for pastries and cakes.
- Plain strong flour for breads and batters.
- Self-raising flour is used for cake making, or a raising agent may be added to soft plain flour.
- All flour must be fresh, dry and sieved to remove all lumps and to incorporate air into the flour.

Sweetening agents

- Caster sugar: dissolves quickly in whisked and creamed mixtures and so is best for sponge cakes.
- Granulated sugar: fine for many plain cakes and fruit cakes.
- Soft brown sugar: gives a rich flavour and colour to fruit cakes and gingerbreads.
- Demerara sugar: a granular texture and only used for biscuits and some cake toppings.
- Icing sugar: used to sprinkle on or dredge cakes and pastries, also for many types of cake icings.
- Golden syrup: sweet and light, used in gingerbreads and 'boiled' cake mixtures, with bicarbonate of soda.
- Black treacle: gives a rich colour to cakes and a distinctive taste, often used with golden syrup.
- Honey: up to one-third of the sugar content may be substituted with honey to give a mellow flavour.

Eggs

- Should be at room temperature to obtain the best results.
- Give colour and flavour to cakes and pastries.
- Will shorten and enrich pastry.
- May be separated. But care must be taken to ensure that the whites are free from any yolk, as the fat from this will lessen the volume of the egg whites when beaten.

Dried fruit

- Raisins, currants and sultanas: should be plump, fresh, moist and clean; any stems should be discarded.
- Candied peel: should be evenly diced and free from any lumps of crystallized sugar.
- Dates: normally in blocks and pre-stoned. They may be chopped easily, and should be sticky not dried and shrivelled up.

- Glacé cherries: very moist and sticky and need to be washed and dried before use in bakery items. This is because the surplus syrup makes them difficult to blend into mixtures, as well as making them heavy and liable to sink while in the mixture.

Fats

- Butter: ideal for light cake mixtures.
- Cake margarine: blended for cake making, has high vegetable oil content.
- Pastry fats: blended for pastries, have a high melting point.
- Lard and margarine: combined for short pastry products.

Methods of Cake Making

Always ensure that the oven is set for the required temperature and that the shelves are suitably positioned. The cake tins should be prepared and ready for use.

By machine

Larger quantities may be mixed by machine than can be successfully made by hand. Always check the maximum machine load before starting to mix. (A U.S. 12 qt mixer takes a 6 lb load.)

Ensure that the correct mixing attachment is fixed to the mixer central spindle. The balloon-shaped whisk is for whisking. The flat beater is for general mixing and creaming. The hook is for the heavier mixing and for kneading doughs. Should it be thought necessary, fix the collar to the bowl before starting to mix the ingredients.

It is essential to use the correct speed for preparing cakes because if too high a speed is used, the texture of the finished cake may be damaged.

Rubbing in
- Incorporate the fat and the flour at minimum speed until the texture of fine breadcrumbs is obtained.
- Add the flavouring ingredients at minimum speed.
- Gradually add liquids while the machine is working at minimum speed until the required consistency is achieved.

Creaming
- Cream the fat and the sugar at a high speed, until it is a light fluffy mixture.
- Switch off the machine and scrape down the bowl. Re-engage the bowl.
- Gradually add half the beaten eggs using a medium speed, then switch off the machine and scrape the bowl down again.

- Using minimum speed, fold in the flour and the remaining eggs alternatively, until they are completely incorporated into a smooth mixture.

Whisking
- Mix the eggs and sugar together using the medium speed, then whisk them using the highest speed until a thick foamy consistency is achieved.
- Turn off the machine and using a hand or a plastic spatula carefully fold in the finely sieved flour. Care needs to be taken here as, if too large a mixture is attempted, this folding-in process can become difficult because of volume involved.

By hand

For best results, ingredients should be at room temperature. Successful mixing/creaming will be achieved if the quantity of ingredients is kept small — to a maximum of 400 g weight.

Rubbing in
- Use the fingertips to incorporate the fat into the sieved flour, before using a wooden spoon to complete the mixing process.
- The fruit should be folded into the mixture after all the other ingredients have been added, to prevent it from being damaged.

Creaming
- The creaming of the fat and sugar may be completed by using the hand (or continuing with a wooden spoon/spatula). The eggs should be well beaten with a fork before they are added to the mixture.
- The eggs and flour should be gradually incorporated into the creamed mixture by adding them alternately, so creating a smooth creamy mixture.

Whisking
- The eggs should be whisked steadily with the sugar over a pan of hot water, until thick and foamy in consistency. (An electric hand-beater/whisk may be used.)
- The finely sieved flour is then carefully folded into the mixture, away from the heat, using a metal spoon and a figure-of-eight movement in the bowl. It creates a very light mixture, full of air.

Whisking egg whites manually

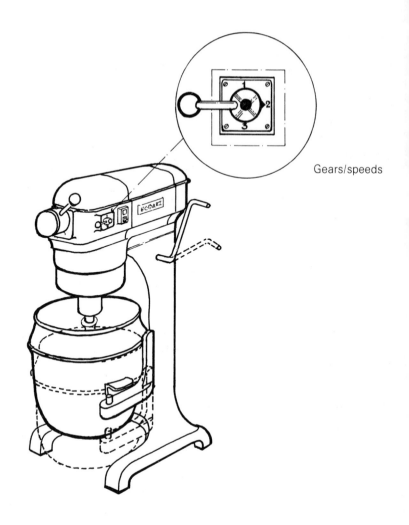

Gears/speeds

Industrial mixing machine

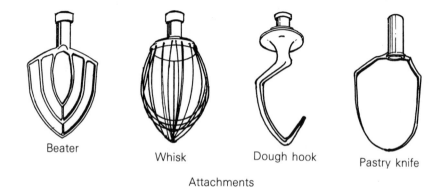

Beater   Whisk   Dough hook   Pastry knife

Attachments

Equipment

Tins, trays, and moulds that are used for bakery need to be treated correctly to prevent any unnecessary damage to their surface or shape. The damage may be caused by:

Scratches: Scraping cooked food particles from the surfaces. The tins and trays should be soaked in warm water to soften the food particles, then they may be gently washed to make them clean.

Warping: This is caused by placing trays into a very hot oven, after bringing them straight from the refrigerator. The contrast of temperature will cause the warping.

Rusting: These items will show signs of rust if they are left in a damp condition. They need to be dried carefully after use and are often placed into an empty hot plate or on a rack above the range to ensure that even the corners are dry.

Denting: This can happen to the smaller items of equipment, such as moulds and cutters. It is caused by poor storage facilities and may be rectified by supplying adequate trays and boxes to enable these small items to be kept in an orderly manner.

Pitting: This can happen to any item that is made from aluminium, it is caused by the use of an alkali such as caustic soda.

Materials used for equipment

Aluminium:
- Sheet aluminium is thin, cheap and is easily bent and warped.
- Cast aluminium is thicker, stronger, and harder and is used for saucepans and some smaller items.

Wood:
- Spoons, rolling pins, chopping boards, sieves and mushrooms are all made of wood. These items all need to be washed carefully to remove the food particles without causing splinters or dents.
- They need to be placed near indirect heat to dry without causing any cracks or warping of the wood.

Steel:
- A hard metal, heavy in weight, that is used for baking sheets. These should be cleaned and then lightly oiled to prevent any rusting.
- Normally stored in the bakery on racks to keep them warm and therefore dry.

Tin:
- This is used for small moulds, tins, cutters, sieves, piping tubes and whisks.
- Tin items must be soaked clean in warm water then dried thoroughly to prevent rust.

Care of equipment

Bakery tins, trays, sheets and moulds should be greased or oiled and lightly dusted with sieved flour to prevent items from sticking to their surfaces. Lard or corn oil are the best commodities to use.

For cakes, the tins need to be lined with greased greaseproof paper to enable the cakes to be baked successfully; the sugar content will make the mixture stick to the surface of the tin. Rich fruit cakes, that need slow cooking for a successful result, should be cooked in a double-lined deep tin with a removable base; these ensure that when cool the cake can be removed from the tin.

 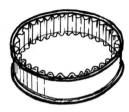 

| Savarin mould | Fluted flan ring | Spring clip cake tin |

Raising Agents

How to make mixtures light

- Sifting — flour and other dry ingredients.
- Rubbing in — incorporating the fat into the flour.
- Whisking — incorporating air into eggs, either whole or just the whites.
- Beating — mixing and creaming fats and sugars together.
- Additions — adding baking powder to mixtures.
- Carbon dioxide — by using yeast to make the mixture rise.
- Layering fat — the steam between the layers makes the pastry rise.

Baking powder

- It is made from one part sodium bicarbonate and two parts cream of tartar.
- In the right conditions it produces carbon dioxide gas. To produce gas a liquid and heat are needed. The majority of gas is released when the mixture is heated.
- Always mix baking powder thoroughly with the sifted flour.
- Keep stored in an airtight container for a short length of time, it does not keep for longer than two months.
- Measure accurately. Excessive baking powder causes cakes to collapse in the centre; insufficient baking powder causes a close heavy texture.

Yeast

- It is a form of plant life and should be used when fresh, moist, crumbly and with a pleasant smell.
- It may be stored for a short length of time (2–3 days) by keeping it well wrapped in a refrigerator.
- Dried yeast may be stored in an airtight container for approximately 3 months. It takes a longer time to cream and is more concentrated than fresh yeast.

The action of heat (and see page 137–8)

Upon yeast:
- The mixture expands during the fermentation process, when carbon dioxide bubbles develop, the yeast cells multiply, and the gluten becomes elastic and soft, creating a honeycomb-textured dough.
- When baked the dough firstly rises, then the yeast is killed by the heat and no further carbon dioxide is produced. The gluten coagulates around the bubbles formed by the gas.

Upon pastry:
- During cooking, steam develops in between the layers of fat and the paste in puff and flaky pastry, thus causing the pastry to rise.

Upon sponges:
- The heat expands the air which is trapped in the mixture and this causes the sponge to rise. The heat sets and cooks the risen mixture to create a light spongy texture.

Types of Cakes

Method	Proportion	Type
Creaming Baked at 180°C	Equal weights of eggs, caster sugar, margarine, flour with baking powder.	*Victoria Sandwich* — two cakes sandwiched together with jam. *Queen cakes* — baked in patty tins with currants in the mixture. *Madeleines* — baked in dariole moulds, covered in jam and coconut to finish.
Rubbed-in Baked at 200°C	1 part flour and baking powder ½ part margarine ⅜ part sugar ⅛ part egg	*Rock cakes* — mixture with currants and spice baked in irregular heaps on baking sheet. *Cherry buns* — mixture with chopped glacé cherries, baked on flat sheet in heaps. *Raspberry buns* — small balls of mixture placed on flat sheet, depress the centre of each cake and fill with raspberry jam before baking.
Whisked Baked at 200°C	1 part egg ½ caster sugar ½ flour	*Swiss roll* — baked in shallow tin, trimmed, and spread with jam, then rolled up. *Sponge flan* — baked in flan-shaped tin, filled with fruit and glazed when cold. *Sponge fingers* — piped onto a lined baking sheet, baked until lightly coloured.
Genoese Baked at 190°C	1 part egg ½ caster sugar ½ flour ¼ butter	*Genoese sponge* — baked in a circular tin with slightly sloping sides. *Chocolate genoese* — cocoa powder added with reduced amount of flour. Decorated with cream and chocolate when cold. *Coffee genoese* — coffee essence added either to the mixture or to the cream filling and iced when the cake is cold.

Types of Pastry

Type	Proportion	Method summary	Dishes/uses
Short-crust Baked at 200°C	½ fat to flour	Fat rubbed into flour to resemble fine breadcrumbs, mixed with cold water to a firm paste.	Jam tarts, small/plate Cornish pasties Quiche Lorraine Baked apple dumpling
Suet-crust	½ suet to flour and baking powder	Mix the shreded suet with the flour and baking powder to a soft dough with water.	Steamed dumplings Steamed suet rolls Steamed meat puddings Steamed fruit puddings
Sugar-paste Baked at 190°C	1 part flour ¼ sugar ⅝ margarine ¼ egg	Cream the egg and sugar together, then gradually add the margarine and the flour, to form a soft paste. Chill before using.	Flan cases that may be baked blind or filled Fruit tartlets Date and apple slice
Full-puff Baked at 225°C	Equal fat to flour, lemon juice	Rub ¼ fat into the flour, mix to a dough with water. Roll to 'star shape' and add rest of fat. Roll and fold 6 times to incorporate the fat. Rest between rolls.	Meat pie crust Sausage rolls Jam puffs Vol au vents Cream horns Vanilla slices
Scotch/ Rough-puff Baked at 220°C	¾ fat to flour, use margarine and lard in equal amounts.	Cut fat to small pieces, mix to a soft lumpy dough with the flour and cold water. Roll and fold to incorporate the fat, 6 times. Rest between rolls.	Meat pie crust Eccles cakes Jalousie Fish pies
Flaky pastry Baked at 220°C	¾ fat to flour	Rub in ¼ fat, mix to a dough with water. Dot on fat in thirds. Roll and fold 6 times. Rest frequently.	Meat pie crust Sausage rolls Jam turnovers
Choux paste Baked at 200°C	¼ litre water 125g flour 100g margarine 4 eggs	Melt fat and boil water in a pan. Beat in flour. Cool. Gradually incorporate eggs, pipe onto greased sheets.	Eclairs Cream buns Profiteroles

Types of Puddings

Type	Proportions	Method summary	Examples
Suet	1 flour ½ suet ¼ sugar	Steam in basin or sleeve. Full steam, 1½–2½ hours. Large or individual sizes.	Steamed sultana pudding Steamed jam roll Steamed ginger pudding
Sponge	1 flour Baking powder ⅔ margarine ⅔ sugar ⅓ egg	• Full steamed — in basin or sleeve, 1–1½ hours. • Baked 175°C in pie dish or tray, or in small individual dishes.	• Chocolate sponge Jam sponge • Eve's pudding Fruit upside-down pudding
Soufflé	1 egg ⅓ butter ⅓ sugar ⅓ flour Milk	Mixture baked in 200°C oven, with the dish in a water-bath to prevent over-heating and curdling. Dariole moulds for individual puddings.	Orange soufflé pudding Lemon soufflé pudding
Egg custard	½ litre milk 3 small eggs 50g sugar	Ingredients whisked up and baked in a greased dish, in a water-bath to prevent the custard curdling. Large or individual.	Baked egg custard Caramel custard Bread and butter pudding Diplomat/cabinet pudding
Fritters	200g flour 10g yeast ¼ litre water	Items floured and then dipped into the well risen batter. Deep fried.	Apple fritters Banana fritters Pineapple fritters
Meringue	50g sugar and 1 egg white	Whisked up, piped onto non-stick paper. Dried out in cool oven.	Meringue chantilly. Meringue nests filled with fruit
Milk pudding	¼ litre milk 50g sugar 50g grain	• Simmered till grain is cooked and pudding thick. • Baked at 200°C until thick.	Rice pudding Semolina pudding Tapioca pudding
Pancakes	¼ litre milk 100g flour 50g sugar 1 egg 10g margarine	Beaten to a smooth batter. Fried in small pan to make thin pancakes, tossed over a quick heat.	Lemon pancakes Apple pancakes Savoury pancakes made if sugar omitted
Junket	½ litre milk 1tsp rennet 10g sugar	Mixed at blood heat then placed into glass dish and left to set.	Junket sprinkled with grated nutmeg

Unit 4 Assessment Activities

1. (a) Name your favourite fruit and collect information about its cultivation.
   (b) Describe ways in which this named fruit can be used in catering.

2. (a) Compile a list of the types of foods that contain nuts.
   (b) Discuss the nutritional value of these foods and suggest similar nutritional products that may be eaten by people who do not like nuts.

3. List types of cakes and biscuits that may be made successfully using one or more of the following ingredients:
   (i) wholemeal flour;
   (ii) Demerara sugar;
   (iii) dark or light Barbados sugar;
   (iv) golden syrup or black treacle.

4. (a) List the types of manual equipment used for pastry work.
   (b) Compile a cleaning schedule for these items.
   (c) Indicate which pieces of equipment are the most difficult to maintain in a clean hygienic condition.

5. (a) Draw a diagram of the electric mixing machine that is used to make pastry items and cakes.
   (b) Indicate the safety procedure that should be followed when using the mixing machine.
   (c) List the types of attachments that are available and give their uses.

Unit 5:

Dairy Produce

Milk
Cream
Oils
Cooking fats
Cheese
Eggs
Methods of cooking eggs
Omelets
Assessment activities

Milk

Milk provides an almost perfect food. Cow's milk contains 87 per cent water, 4 per cent protein, 3.5 per cent fat, 4 per cent carbohydrate, and vitamins A, B, C, and D as well as minerals.

Facts
- The protein in 500 ml milk equals that found in 3 eggs, or 100g of red meat or white fish.
- The calcium content in 500 ml equals that found in 75g of Cheddar cheese.
- The calories found in 500 ml milk equals that found in 500g white fish, 4 eggs, or 125g fried steak.

Apart from supplying an almost completely balanced food, milk provides an almost perfect base for the growth of bacteria; for this reason the utmost care is taken to ensure hygienic conditions of storage and use of milk. With the exception of a small quantity of farm-bottled milk, all milk sold in the UK is tuberculin tested.

Storage
- Fresh milk should be kept in clean containers, covered, and in a refrigerator or very cool area, for 24 hours, maximum.
- Fresh milk should be kept well away from any sunlight as this will destroy the vitamin C content and encourage the milk to turn sour.
- UHT and sterilized milk may be kept in a cool storage area for a maximum of three months until it is unsealed; it should then be stored as fresh milk.
- Evaporated and condensed milk is canned and may be stored in a cool airy storeroom for a number of years without deterioration taking place. Once opened, it should be placed in a refrigerator and used within 24 hours.
- Dried milk should be stored carefully. It will become easily contaminated by airborne bacteria and insects unless it is kept in airtight containers, in a cool store-room.
- Dried milk should be purchased in sealed bags in a size that will ensure that once the bag is unsealed it may be used within a few weeks to ensure its freshness.
- Cream should be stored in a refrigerator and used within 24 hours. It must be kept away from all pungent-smelling foods.
- UHT and sterilized creams should be stored in the same way as milks preserved in this manner.
- Synthetic cream powder should be stored with as much care as dried milk. It is very susceptible to contamination and can be a dangerous commodity to store for any length of time. It should be in small sealed cartons or packets and kept cool and dry until used. Care should be paid to the use-by date on the packets.

Types of Milk

Treatment	Method summary	Characteristics and uses
Pasteurized	Held at 82°C for 15 secs then cooled to 4°C.	Bottled — silver foil top. A definite cream line visible. Suitable for normal uses. 48 hour maximum life in a refrigerator.
Homogenized	The fat globules are dispersed throughout the milk. Then pasteurised.	Bottled — red foil top. Cream is evenly distributed thoughout the milk. Ideal for catering uses. 48 hour life if cool and kept in refrigerator.
Channel Island	Pasteurized. From Channel Island herds, 4 per cent minimum fat content.	Bottled — gold foil top. Expensive, and not used in catering units. Very rich and creamy.
Sterilized	Homogenized then placed in bottles and heated to 104°C and held for 30 minutes.	In tall hermetically-sealed bottles. Will keep for 3 months unopened. A very definite flavour change due to the heat treatment. Not used in catering trade.
Ultra Heat Treatment	Homogenized then heated to 130°C for 1 second. Packed into sterile cartons and cooled.	Unopened cartons will keep for 6 months. A definite cooked flavour. Individual cartons are used extensively for the service of tea in catering outlets.
Evaporated	60 per cent of the water is removed, it is a thick liquid sterilized then canned. Rich in flavour.	Available in small-sized cans only as it has a short life once opened. A very rich creamy taste. It may be used as it is or reconstituted by adding water.
Condensed	Over 60 per cent of the water is removed, then it is pasteurized and canned. May be sweetened.	A very thick creamy consistency. Not often used in the catering trade. Packed into small cans. May be used to make fudge toppings.
Dried	Roller or spray dried. A powder or granular form of milk. Usually from skimmed milk, so it has a low fat level.	Packed in airtight containers. Concentrated nutrients and high in protein. It is best to reconstitute small amounts as required, once reconstituted it has a maximum of 12 hours shelf life.

Types of Cream

Type	Milk treatment summary	Characteristics and uses
Coffee	Homogenized and then pasteurized.	15 per cent fat content. Used with coffee and will not whip. Keeps for 24 hours in refrigerator. Thin consistency.
Single	Homogenized and then pasteurized.	A thicker cream that has 25 per cent fat content. Used for enriching sauces and soups. Keeps for 24 hours in refrigerator.
Double	Homogenized and then pasteurized.	Has 59 per cent fat content and is a thick pouring consistency that will whip to an even thicker cream, to be piped and used to decorate cakes and sweets. Keeps for 24 hours in refrigerator.
Clotted	It is gently heated to 82°C and the resulting thick cream at the surface is skimmed off and then cooled as rapidly as possible.	Has 65 per cent fat content. A very thick, slightly lumpy cream. Used for service of scones and cakes, it may not be whipped or piped. It may be served to accompany compote of fruit. It will keep for 24 hours in a cold part of a refrigerator.
UHT	Homogenized and then heated to 132°C for 1 second, put into cartons and cooled.	A thin cream frequently packed into individual cartons and used in fast-food outlets for service of coffee. It will keep for 6 months if unopened.
UHT whipped	UHT treated then put into aerosol cans and cooled	A whipped product that will pipe directly onto foods but will only stay whipped for 15 seconds. Limited use in catering outlets.
Sterilized	Sterilized and canned, or put into jars and sealed.	A thick cream with a cooked taste. A rich cream colour. Will keep well if unopened. Limited catering use.
Synthetic	Dehydrated. Found in a powder or granular form.	The powder is blended with water then whipped to produce a thick cream that may be piped. Must be used as soon as reconstituted as it is susceptible to bacterial infection.

Oils

Types of Oils

Type	Characteristics	Uses	Temperatures
Olive	The most expensive, has a distinctive flavour. Produced from the olive fruit.	Vinaigrette Mayonnaise	Flash point 270°C Smoke point 148°C
Groundnut	A popular oil readily available. Produced from ground nuts.	Deep frying	Flash point 200°C Smoke point 230°C
Maize/ corn	A medium priced oil with a golden colour. Very little flavour.	Deep frying Baking Cold sauces	Flash point 360°C Smoke point 232°C
Vegetable	An inexpensive oil — blended. Safe for frying as it has a high flash point and a low smoke point.	Deep frying Oiling tins and trays for pastry products and cakes	Flash point 320°C Smoke point 230°C

Safety points for oils

Oils will go rancid if they are stored in a warm atmosphere. Because of their relatively low flash points they should be stored in a cool place, well away from naked flames or heated equipment. If refrigerated they may congeal; however, they readily revert to their fluid state when warmed.

Quality and storage points

- Oils should be clear, with a pouring consistency and even colour. Free from any visible particles. Fresh smelling.
- Oils should be stored in sealed containers in cool airy place and used in stock rotation.
- Oils must be kept free from moisture as water content will cause them to splutter when heated.
- Fats (oils solid at room temperature) should be smooth and should smell fresh. There should be no variation in their colour.
- All fats should be stored in a refrigerator and used in stock rotation, as they will go rancid if stale.

Types of Animal Fats

Type	Origin	Characteristics	Uses
Lard	Pig's fat rendered down.	White smooth soft fat. Low melting point. Long shelf life.	Hot water paste, greasing tins and trays, pastry, shallow frying and roasting
Suet	Beef, hard fat from around the kidneys.	Hard solid fat that is shredded and dusted with rice flour to keep it free flowing. Cream colour.	Suet paste Christmas mincemeat Dumplings Steamed puddings
Dripping	Rendered fat from animals — beef, pork.	A semi-hard fat with the flavour of the meat that it originates from. Sandy white colour.	Shallow frying meat items Roasting meats and vegetables Brown roux and sauces
Butter	Churned from milk fat.	A creamy smooth pale yellow fat that may be salted or unsalted. Rich in vitamins A and D.	Shallow frying uncoated fish. Parsley butter and brandy butter. Spread on toast and scones. Genoese sponge. Hollandaise sauce

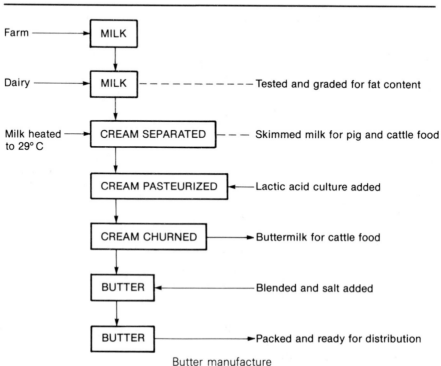

Butter manufacture

Types of Vegetable Fats

These are manufactured from varying quantities of whole cream, milk, and vegetable oils. Vitamins A and D and a slight colouring agent are added to margarine to increase its acceptance as an alternative to animal fats.

Type	Characteristics	Uses
Block margarine	May be either a hard or semi-hard fat.	White roux and sauces Pastry and basic cakes
Table margarine	A soft fat sold in tubs, or boxes. Substitute for butter.	Used for sandwiches Butter icings and some creamed cake mixtures.
Pastry margarine	A semi-hard fat blended especially for pastry making.	Pastries
Vegetable cooking fat	A white smooth semi-hard blended fat.	Most cooking processes Substitute for lard

Note: The conversion of liquid oils to solid fats is called 'oil hardening' and is done by a process known as *hydrogenation*.

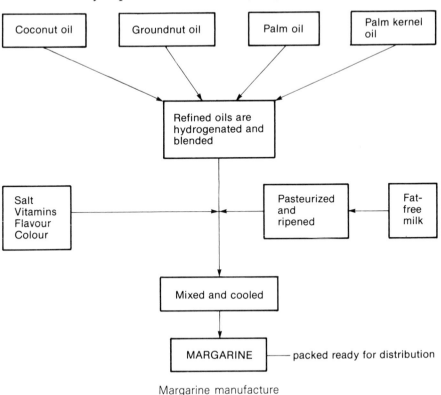

Margarine manufacture

Cheese

Manufacture

The milk is clotted by the addition of rennet and turns to curds and whey. The curd is cut and pressed together. The whey is drained off and used for pig rearing. The curds are then pressed into moulds and stored while they mature.

Quality

There should be no signs of any mould or mildew. There should be no dry cracks or fat globules on the surface. The cheese should smell pleasant. Soft cheese should not be runny.

Uses of cheese in the kitchen

Cheese will increase the protein content of the meal and will add variety of flavour. It can be used in the following ways:

Grilling
- The cheese is grated finely and then sprinkled upon foods that are to be grilled, often to finish off the dish just before service.
- Used in fish dishes, with eggs, in potato dishes, on pizza.

Baking
- The hard cheese is as dry as possible and grated finely; it should have a strong flavour. It is added to the pastry, with seasoning, before any liquid is added.
- Examples are scones, savoury flans, and cheese straws.

Sauces
- The dry, strongly flavoured cheese is added to the completed sauce, finely grated, and *not* allowed to re-boil. Good seasoning is essential to produce an acceptable sauce.
- Mornay sauce used with fish, eggs, and pasta.

Frying
- Finely grated cheese is added to dishes such as omelets and fritters, just before they are cooked.
- Sliced cheese is used in fast food outlets, such as those serving cheeseburgers.

Flavouring
- Cheese is grated with salads, used in Welsh rarebit, pasta dishes, and with soups, as a secondary flavour.

Snacks
- It is extensively used to provide filled bread rolls and sandwiches and for toasted snacks.

Cheeseboards
- Good selection of cheeses.
- Variety of flavours, textures, and colours.
- Garnishes to enhance the presentation and taste.
- Crisp biscuits and firm butter served with the cheese.

Care should be taken with cheese because:
- Small quantities of cheese are used to encourage the flow of digestive juices but the flavour should not always be allowed to dominate the dish.
- Due to the high fat content, cheese may prove difficult to digest unless it is chopped, or grated, and chewed well before being swallowed.
- If over-heated, the cheese will become increasingly difficult to digest, as the heat will melt the fat content and the protein will become hard.
- When producing dishes that have to be gratinated, a very hot salamander should be used to ensure the desired browning effect without making the cheese indigestible.
- When adding cheese to sauces it should be finely grated and mixed into the very hot sauce. No further boiling should take place as this will cause the cheese protein to harden, the cheese fat to separate, and make the resulting mixture very difficult to digest.

English cheese

Hard cheeses include the following:
Cheddar: Yellow or red in colour. Buttery and mellow. Used for many cheese dishes. Cooks well.
Cheshire: Mellow flavoured, white, loose texture, crumbly and mild. Used on its own on a cheeseboard, too mild for cooking.
Gloucester: Pale orange colour, close crumbly cheese with a medium strength flavour.
Caerphilly: Has a short shelf-life. White, with a mild delicate flavour, used on cheeseboard.
Derby: A mild cheese with a close texture and pale colour. May have sage added for variety of flavour and colour.
Lancashire: A mellow crumbly yellow cheese.
Leicester: A deep orange, mild, mellow flavoured cheese, loose and flaky texture.
Wensleydale: White, soft, creamy, mild cheese, used for cheeseboards.

English blue vein cheeses:
Stilton: A thick crust and a well-veined interior.
Lymeswold: A flat shape and a thin crust; soft cheese.
Wensleydale: Soft, mild flavour; in short supply.
Cheshire: Blue veined with a mild flavour.

Foreign Cheeses

	Country	Type	Characteristics
HARD	Switzerland	Emmental	Large gas holes, pale yellow cheese, hard waxy texture.
	Switzerland	Gruyère	Small gas holes, pale yellow colour, hard waxy texture.
	Holland	Edam	Small and round with a red waxed skin, hard yellow cheese with rubbery texture.
	Holland	Gouda	Pale yellow, flat, disc-shaped, yellow wax skin.
	Italy	Parmesan	Very hard, deep yellow-coloured cheese. Very pungent aroma and flavour. Used grated to sprinkle upon foods, never on a cheeseboard.
SEMI-HARD	France	St Paulin	A mild, round, spongy textured cheese.
	France	Pont-l'Évêque	A square-shaped, soft curd cheese with a thin yellow rind.
	Italy	Bel Paese	A mild, round cheese, with a spongy texture.
SOFT	France	Camembert	A light floury rind, creamy runny consistency. Mild flavour.
	France	Brie	A full creamy runny cheese with a firm rind. Mild flavour.
	France	Carré de L'Est	A square-shaped creamy cheese.
	France	Pommel demi-sel	A white creamy croquette-shaped cheese.
BLUE VEIN	France	Roquefort	A soft creamy crumbly cheese. Rich and pungent flavour.
	Italy	Gorgonzola	Semi-hard, crumbly, blue mould. Strong pungent flavour.
	Danish	Danish Blue	A soft, slightly salty cheese. High fat content

Storage of foreign cheeses

Because they have been imported into the UK foreign cheeses must be chosen with care to ensure that they are ripe. They should then be served immediately, not kept.

Eggs

Eggs are graded into standard sizes:
    Size 1 = 70 grams ⎫
    Size 2 = 65 grams ⎬ large grade eggs
    Size 3 = 60 grams ⎭
    Size 4 = 55 grams ⎫ standard grade eggs
    Size 5 = 50 grams ⎭
    Size 6 = 45 grams — medium grade eggs
    Size 7 = 40 grams and below — small grade eggs
Class A eggs are the freshest quality eggs available.
Class B eggs are less fresh.

Storage of eggs

Eggs should be stored in a cool place, 1–5°C, and should be used in strict rotation. The crates should be kept on slatted shelves well above floor level. Care should be taken to eliminate the danger of cracking or breaking the eggs whilst still in the crates. As the shells are porous the egg will easily absorb odours and must therefore be kept well away from strong smelling foods. The pointed end should be placed downwards in the tray, so as to allow the air sac in the egg to be uppermost.

Nutritional value

Eggs provide the following nutrients: protein; fat; iron and phosphorous; and vitamins A, B and D.

Freshness

There are various methods of determining the freshness of an egg:
• A fresh smell should be apparent when the shell is broken.
• The white of the egg should be thick and clear.
• The yolk of the egg should be in the centre of the white.
• The air sac at the rounded end of the egg should be small in size.
• A fresh egg will sink to the bottom of a saline solution.

Preservation of eggs

Dried — The beaten eggs are either film- or spray-dried, so that they may be stored and used at a later date. They are easily reconstituted for use but this liquid egg is liable to become contaminated and should therefore be used immediately. It is often used in the manufacture of sponge mixes and other convenience products.
Frozen — Beaten eggs are frozen and sold by liquid volume — by the litre.

Uses

Hens' eggs have the following uses in cooking:
Thickening — for custards and sauces, and baked egg custards. The mixture will over-heat and curdle very easily, so a water-bath is often used.
Binding — for croquettes, fish cakes, and all types of stuffings used with meats and fish.
Coating — with breadcrumbs, for foods that may otherwise disintegrate while cooking.
Glazing — for pastries of all types, to give the surface a golden brown colour when it is cooked.
Enriching — also for flavouring foods. The addition of an egg to foods will give an increased nutritional value. Egg may be added to pastry, potato dishes, and sauces.
Lightening — whisking incorporates air into mixtures such as meringues, soufflés, sponges, creams and gâteaux.
Garnishing — hard-boiled eggs are often diced or sieved and then used to garnish dishes, or they may be halved and the whites used as shells into which a flavoured filling can be piped, for a larger garnish.
Emulsifier — the egg is beaten and used in the making of mayonnaise and other egg-based sauces where the egg itself holds the ingredients in suspension.

Thickening

Binding

Coating

Glazing

Enriching

Lightening

Garnishing

Emulsifier

Cooking of Eggs

Type	Method summary	Service
Scrambled eggs *Oeufs brouillés*	Cook the beaten eggs in a thick-based pan, with a knob of butter, over a gentle heat, stirring until the mixture is set.	The egg mixture is placed onto hot buttered toast and served immediately.
Cocotte eggs *Oeufs en cocotte*	Break the eggs into a buttered cocotte dish and place in a shallow pan with simmering water. Allow the egg to cook slowly with a lid on the pan; it should be just set.	The cocotte dish is cleaned, and placed on a 15cm plate with a doily. Served immediately.
Hard-boiled eggs *Oeufs dur*	Whole eggs are cooked in fast boiling water for 8 minutes. To cool they are placed into cold running water.	The shell is removed when the egg is cold. It is often halved and filled for service.
Fried eggs *Oeufs frits*	Gently break the eggs into a frying pan with hot fat. Cook until the egg is just set.	The egg is drained well and served with fried bacon and toast.
Soft-boiled eggs *Oeufs mollets*	The whole egg is cooked in a pan of simmering water for 3½−4 minutes. It is served immediately.	The egg may be shelled and coated with sauce, or placed in an egg cup for service.
Poached eggs *Oeufs pochés*	The egg is gently broken into a shallow pan of simmering water with a drop of vinegar. it is cooked slowly until just set, then drained well.	Served on trimmed hot buttered toast. Or it may be coated with a sauce and served in an earthenware dish.
Fried/grilled eggs *Oeufs sur le plat*	Break the egg into a buttered shallow individual egg dish, place on the edge of the range until the egg is set on the base. Finish quickly under the hot grill until just set but not coloured at all by the heat.	The dish is cleaned and placed on a dish paper on a flat silver serving dish. It should be served immediately.

Omelets

Preparation and cooking

Allow 2 or 3 eggs per omelet. Always use very fresh eggs and fry in best butter. The omelet pan should be a thick-based pan with a well-angled handle and sloping sides 3 or 3.5cm high. It should be used for the cooking of omelets only as the surface is easily damaged and this makes the turning out of the omelets very difficult. Care should be taken when cleaning omelet pans. They should be wiped out while still hot and never scoured out or scratched.

Basic method

Beat the eggs with a fork, and then pour into a pan containing foaming melted butter. Cook quickly over a fierce heat until the mixture is lightly set, shaking the pan all the time. Next, half-fold the omelet and tilt the pan to enable the omelet to fold out onto a heated silver flat. Serve all omelets immediately, they will spoil if kept hot.
  Basic omelets include the following:
- *Omelette aux fines herbes* — add a pinch of parsely, chervil and chives to the mixture.
- *Omelette aux champignons* — sauté sliced mushrooms then cook the omelet in the same pan.
- *Omelette au fromage* — add grated cheese just before folding the omelet.

Flat method

Cook as for a basic omelet then, when set, toss as for a pancake, turn out onto a heated flat dish and serve immediately.
  For example:
- *Omelette paysanne* — diced fried potato, onion and bacon are placed into the pan, then the omelet is cooked in that pan.
- *Omelette fermière* — chopped parsely is added before the egg mixture is cooked to an omelet.

Unit 5 Assessment Activities

1. (a) List recipes that may be made with the use of dried milk powder in the following categories: soup; sauces; puddings; pastry items; cakes.
   (b) Make a half litre of custard sauce using dried milk and the same quantity using fresh pasteurised milk. Compare the results in terms of: (i) cost; (ii) preparation time; (iii) taste.

2. Shallow fry potato slices in: olive oil; corn oil; vegetable oil. Compare and discuss the results in terms of: (i) cost; (ii) taste; (iii) odour and fumes.

3. (a) Draw up plans for a cheese promotion week at a place of your choice.
   (b) List the types of cheese that will be included and name ways of increasing the use of cheese during the promotion week.

4. Draw a map of England with the main cities marked, indicating the types of cheeses that are produced in England and their production areas.

5. (a) Compile a list of dishes that may be made with the use of English Cheddar cheese.
   (b) List the nutrients that will be present in 5 of the dishes that you have listed.

Unit 6:

Fish and Meat

Types of Fish

Because of the availability of frozen fish of all types and sizes, it is now possible to use good quality fish at all times of the year. Fish are classified as follows:

White round	White flat	Oily	Crustacea	Mollusca
Cod	Plaice	Herring	Lobster	Oyster
Whiting	Sole	Mackerel	Crab	Mussels
Hake	Turbot	Salmon		

Nutritional value

- White fish contain first-class protein, with vitamins A and D present in the liver.
- Oily fish also contain first-class protein, with some fat/oil and vitamins A and D.

Purchasing

Prepared fish should be purchased by weight/number of portions, for example, 20 plaice fillets at 75g per fillet, thus enabling the caterer to ensure that each portion will be the same cost and size.

	Quality	Storage
Fresh fish	Bright eyes and red gills. Pleasant smell. Flesh firm and scales moist.	Minimum time. On trays of ice and in separate refrigerator.
Frozen fish	In sealed bags or containers. No damaged or whitened flesh. Fish not chipped or broken. Clearly labelled, indicating type and size of contents.	In sealed containers in deep freeze unit. Use in stock rotation. Never re-freeze after thawing

Method of purchase	Appropriate uses
Whole, gutted with or without head	Large-scale: buffets, banquets Small-scale: à la carte menus
Fillets, cutlets, steaks — block or free-flow	Known numbers in welfare, industrial use. In small numbers for à la carte menus
Fillets and portions — battered, oven-ready — battered, to deep fry — egg and crumbed —in sauce	Known service time and limited frying equipment. Small numbers; bar snacks; fast food. Fast food, industrial, medium numbers. Microwave/ vending, 24 hour service.
Fingers — breaded or battered Cakes — breaded	Children's meals, school meals. Industrial, welfare, school meals.
Balls — in batter Scampi — in crumbs or batter	Fast food and bar snacks. Bar snacks, fast food.
Prawns — free-flow Crab meat	Sauces, hors d'oeuvres, salads. Hors d'oeuvres

Cuts of fish

Whole
- Large fish, such as whole salmon, may be poached and, when cold, decorated and used as centre pieces for buffets.
- Small fish, such as plaice and sole, may be poached, grilled, or fried and served hot.

Fillets
- Filleted fish, such as plaice, haddock, and herrings, may be poached, grilled or fried, either as they are or with a coating of batter, egg and breadcrumbs, seasoned flour, or oatmeal.

Delice
- Quarter or small fillets may be folded and poached, then coated in a sauce.
- Examples of fish used include plaice, sole and haddock.

Goujons
- Cut from the fillet, these are strips 6cm to 0.5cm in size. They are floured, egg and breadcrumbed and deep fried.

Suprême
- Fillets of large fish, cut on the slant, such as turbot; usually poached or grilled.

Paupiette
- Fillet of fish, spread with stuffing then rolled up and gently baked in a moderate oven.

Tronçon
- A slice from a flat fish, cut on the bone, for example, turbot. May be grilled or poached.

Darne
- A slice of round fish cut on the bone, often called a cutlet, such as from cod or salmon. May be poached or baked.

Methods of Cooking Fish

- *Boiling:* Gently cook the fish in plenty of liquid. Whole fish should be placed in cold water and brought slowly to the boil to prevent the flesh from breaking up. Rapid boiling will damage the fish.
- *Poaching:* Scarcely cover the pieces of fish with liquid. Cover the dish with greaseproof paper and cook in a moderate oven. If the liquid is allowed to boil rapidly the flesh will break up.
- *Grilling:* The fish is passed through seasoned flour, brushed with oil, then placed on a greased baking sheet and grilled under a moderate heat. The fish should be turned over once only.
- *Shallow frying:* The fish is passed through seasoned flour and then gently fried in shallow fat. The presentation side should be fried first. The fish is only turned once. Some fish is prepared with a coating of flour, egg and breadcrumbs prior to frying.
- *Deep frying:* The fish is coated with either flour, egg, and bread-crumbs, or in a frying batter. The fat should be at the correct temperature before the fish is lowered carefully onto the fryer, one piece at a time. It is not possible to use a basket as the fish will tend to stick to the mesh. A 'spider' (a long-handled draining implement) is used to remove the cooked fish from the fryer. All deep-fried fish must be drained well to remove any excess fat. It will not keep hot for many minutes without losing its crispness, it should therefore be served immediately.

One method of coating a fish for deep frying is called *pané*, when the fish is passed through seasoned flour, egg and breadcrumbs (see below).

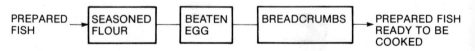

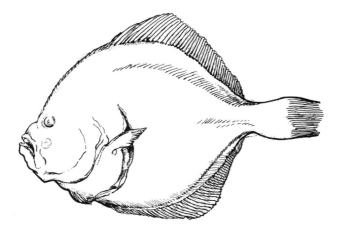

'Flat' fish (turbot)   approx. 1/10 full size

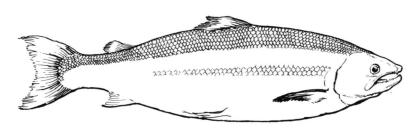

'Round' fish   approx. 1/8 full size

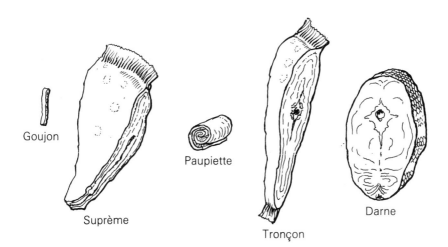

Goujon

Suprème

Paupiette

Tronçon

Darne

Cuts of fish

Fish Dishes

Dish	Method summary	Accompaniments
Shallow fried fish *Poisson meunière*	Whole or filleted fish passed through seasoned flour, shallow fried.	Lemon slices. Browned butter. Sprinkled with chopped parsley
Grilled cod steaks *Darne de cabillaud grillé*	Steaks passed through seasoned flour and grilled.	Slice of lemon. sprig of parsley or parsley butter.
Grilled fillets of plaice *Filets de plie grillés*	Fillets passed through seasoned flour and grilled	Slice of lemon. Sprig of parsley/parsley butter
Fried whiting *Merlan frit*	Fish floured, egg and crumbed, then deep fried.	Fried parsley. Tartare sauce. Lemon wedge.
Fried fillets of plaice *Filets de plie frits*	Fillets floured, egg and crumbed, deep fried.	Lemon wedge. Parsley sprig. Tartare sauce.
Deep-fried fish in batter *Poisson frit à l'Orly*	Marinated in oil and lemon. Floured and dipped in batter, deep fried.	Parsley sprigs. Hot tomato sauce served separately.
Whitebait *Blanchailles*	Passed through milk and seasoned flour. Deep fried, drained well.	Fried parsley. Quarters of lemon.
Boiled cod *Cabillaud poché*	Darnes (slices on the bone)/fillets, simmered in lemon and salt water.	Served with parsley or anchovy or egg sauce.
Sole fillets with velouté sauce, tomato and parsley *Filets de sole Dugléré*	Fillets baked in oven with tomato concassé, white wine and parsley.	Served coated with velouté sauce.
Sole fillets with grapes and fish velouté *Filets de sole Veronique*	Fillets poached with white wine, lemon and shallots.	Served coated glazed, and garnished with grapes.
Fillets with mornay sauce *Filets de sole Mornay*	Fillets poached in fish stock.	Served coated with sauce and gratinated.

Preservation of Fish

Preservation	Fish	Method summary	Uses
Smoked	Haddock	Slit open. Salted then smoked.	Poached in milk — breakfast. Kedgeree.
	Herring	Lightly salted then smoked for 6 hours.	Whole — bloater — grilled, served with parsley butter. Split — kipper — poached or grilled, served with melted butter.
	Salmon	Filleted, salted, rinsed then smoked.	Whole or in very thin slices. Hors d'oeuvres. Canapés. Sandwiches.
	Mackerel	Filleted then salted and smoked.	Fillets are served with lettuce as an hors d'oeuvre, with lemon wedges as a garnish.
	Trout	The fish is gutted then smoked.	Trout are served as an hors d'oeuvre on a bed of crisp lettuce.
Canned	Sardines	Canned in oil or tomato sauce.	Savouries on toast, sandwich fillings. Salads.
	Pilchards	Canned in tomato sauce.	Snack meals, served on toast. Made into fish cakes and pies.
	Mackerel	Canned in brine.	Hors d'oeuvres and salads.
	Tuna	Canned in own juice.	Fish pies, cakes and salads.
	Salmon	Canned in own juice.	Salads and sandwich fillings. Fish pies, cakes, flans, snack meals.
	Shrimps	Canned in brine.	Sauces, salads, appetisers.
	Prawns	Canned in brine.	Salads, open sandwiches, appetisers.
	Mixed oily fish	Pâte	Hors d'oeuvres. Open sandwiches.
Bottled	Shrimps	Potted	Hors d'oeuvres. Salads.
	Mixed oily fish	Paste	Sandwiches, filled rolls, snacks.

Meat

Because of the high proportion of the caterer's budget that is spent upon meat, it is essential to be able to produce acceptable profitable dishes from each cut of the carcass. The hindquarter and backbone area will produce the fine grain joints as these parts of the animal have not used their muscles much. Young animals will produce fine grain lean cuts, as the muscle fibres are still short in length. Large animals, such as beef cattle, will provide some joints from the fore-quarter and lower leg parts of the carcass that have long muscle fibres, due to the perpetual movements of these muscle areas during the lifetime of the cattle. The joints/cuts with short fine grain muscles will be successfully cooked by quick methods, such as grilling, frying and roasting. Those joints/cuts that are composed of long muscle fibres will require slower moist methods of cooking, such as braising, stewing and boiling.

Nutritional value

Meat has a high protein content and also contains fat and vitamin B.

Composition of meat

- Made up of bundles of muscle fibres, held together with connective tissue.
- Fat may be present around the edge of a joint or marbled between the lean.

Storage of meat

- **Carcass** and large joints should be hung in a refrigerator. Care must be taken to prevent the blood from dripping onto any other commodity.
- **Small cuts** and joints should be placed on separate clean trays in the refrigerator and lightly covered to prevent evaporation of the natural moisture.
- **Frozen meats** should be kept below $0°C$ in a deep freeze unit or placed on a clean tray in the refrigerator to thaw out before being cooked.
- **Sliced cooked meat** must be placed on trays and covered to keep fresh; it must be kept in the refrigerator at all times.
- **Cooked meat** (in sauce) must be cooled rapidly and placed in the refrigerator. It must be kept very cold.

Meat definitions

- **Collagen:** White connective tissue that holds the bundles of fibres together. It changes its composition when cooked with moisture to form gelatine.
- **Elastin:** Yellow inedible connective tissue that is present down the neck and back area of the carcass. It is seen on cuts such as chops and cutlets and should be trimmed away before the meat is cooked.
- **Spinal cord:** A soft grey/white tubular substance found between the spinal bones. Found in chops and cutlets, it should be removed before the meat is cooked.
- **Extractives:** The juices found in lean meat that are responsible for the flavour. These juices are squeezed out if the meat is over-cooked by excessive heat. In moist cooking methods, such as braised or stewed dishes, they flavour the gravy.

Bacon

Bacon is the cured flesh of a baconer pig, which is especially bred to produce a carcass with a very long back and a small layer of fat.

Nutritional value	Origin	Quality	Storage
Protein Fat Vitamin B	Britain Denmark	No unpleasant smell or stickiness on the surface White smooth fat Pink lean flesh Fine fibres	Sides are wrapped in muslin and hung in a cool storeroom. Sliced on covered trays.

Types of bacon

- **Smoked bacon** This is salted, either by the dry method or soaked in brine. The carcass is then smoked. Smoked bacon has a stronger flavour than green bacon. It also keeps better.
- **Green bacon** The carcass is cured in brine. Green bacon has a very mild flavour and a short shelf life.

Cuts	Method of cooking	Uses/accompaniments
1. Collar	Boil. Rashers — fried.	Boiled bacon and pease pudding.
2. Hock	Boil. Diced in pies.	Savoury pies or flans.
3. Streaky	Rashers. Bacon rolls.	Used in savoury flans.
4. Back	Rashers — grilled or fried.	With eggs, sausage, tomato.
5. Gammon	Boil. Slices — grilled.	Grilled gammon and pineapple.
6. Through-cut	Rashers — cut using the whole side of bacon, streaky and back.	Grilled or fried.

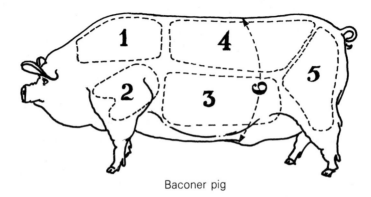

Baconer pig

Beef

Quality points

- The lean should be a bright red and marbled.
- The fat should be firm, brittle and creamy white. It should smell fresh.

Storage

- The carcass is hung in an atmosphere of $1°C$ to increase the tenderness of the meat.
- Cuts of meat should be placed on trays and kept moist, and away from other meats. They should be well drained, not lying in blood.

Nutritional value

Beef, which comes from England and Scotland, contains much protein, and also fat, phosphorus, iron, and vitamin B.

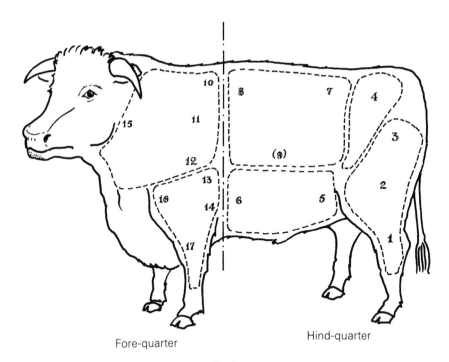

Fore-quarter

Hind-quarter

Beef

	Cuts	Cooking method
Hind-quarter	1. *Shin*	Mince. Soup.
	2. *Silverside*	Salted, boiled. Braise.
	3. *Topside*	Second-class roast. Braise.
	4. *Rump*	Roast. Steaks — fried.
	5. *Thick flank*	Braise.
	6. *Thin flank*	Stew. Sausages. Mince.
	7. *Sirloin*	Roast. Steaks — fried.
	8. *Wing rib*	Roast.
	9. *Fillet*	Roast. Steaks — grilled.
Fore-quarter	10. *Fore rib*	Second-class roast. Braise.
	11. *Middle rib*	Braise. Pies. Puddings.
	12. *Chuck rib*	Stew. Pies. Puddings.
	13. *Plate*	Mince. Sausages.
	14. *Brisket*	Salted, boiled, pressed.
	15. *Sticking*	Mince. Sausages.
	16. *Leg of mutton*	Stewed.
	17. *Shank*	Soup. Mince. Beef tea.

BEEF

Method of cooking	Method of service	Accompaniments
Boiled	Sliced onto a silver flat with turned carrots and whole onions.	Dumplings. The boiling liquor served separately.
Stewed	In an earthenware dish with turned root vegetables to garnish.	Dumplings. Chopped parsley sprinkled on top.
Braised	Placed on a flat dish with button onions and julienne of root vegetables to garnish.	Piped duchesse border around the dish. Ribbon of sauce, from braise.
Roast	Sliced onto a silver flat dish. Roast potatoes placed around the edge. A ribbon of roast gravy.	Yorkshire pudding. Horseradish sauce and roast gravy served separately.
Fried/grilled steaks	Placed on a silver flat with onion rings, grilled tomatoes, and button mushrooms.	Green salad. Watercress. Mustard offered separately. Straw potatoes.
Minced beef	Used in various made-up dishes such as pies, pasties, and pasta-based items.	Well-seasoned sauce.
Sausages	Placed on a flat dish with fried eggs, bacon, mushrooms, and tomatoes.	Croûtes of bread, or sauté potatoes. Watercress.
Consommé	In warmed consommé cup, and saucer.	Consommé garnish. Toast. See page 39.
Beef tea	In warmed soup bowl.	Bread rolls
Puddings	Served in a cleaned basin with a starched napkin folded around.	Gravy from the meat served separately.
Pies	Cleaned pie dish with a pie collar placed on a silver flat.	Gravy from meat served separately.
Burgers	In a toasted bun with onion and pickle.	French fried potatoes. Green salad.

Beef Steaks

Fillet

Using the whole fillet in the following manner creates maximum use and profitability from what is the most expensive cut of beef.

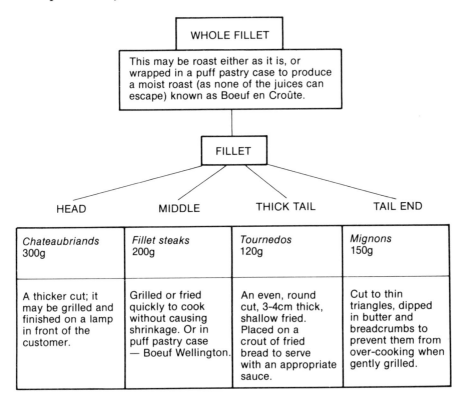

WHOLE FILLET
This may be roast either as it is, or wrapped in a puff pastry case to produce a moist roast (as none of the juices can escape) known as Boeuf en Croûte.

FILLET

HEAD	MIDDLE	THICK TAIL	TAIL END
Chateaubriands 300g	*Fillet steaks* 200g	*Tournedos* 120g	*Mignons* 150g
A thicker cut; it may be grilled and finished on a lamp in front of the customer.	Grilled or fried quickly to cook without causing shrinkage. Or in puff pastry case — Boeuf Wellington.	An even, round cut, 3-4cm thick, shallow fried. Placed on a crout of fried bread to serve with an appropriate sauce.	Cut to thin triangles, dipped in butter and breadcrumbs to prevent them from over-cooking when gently grilled.

Sirloin

- Porterhouse/T-bone steak.
  Steaks cut through the bone from the sirloin joint, including the fillet.
- Sirloin steak.
  Cut into 1.5cm slices, 150g in weight. These slices are without the bone or the fillet.
- Minute steak.
  Cut into 1cm slices with no bone or fillet. Tenderised and flattened into a thin steak.

Rump

- Rump steak is cut from the top part of the rump joint into 1.5cm slices, tenderised and fried.

Cooking steaks

Steaks are seasoned on both sides and brushed with oil and butter. They are placed on a hot grill tray or bars and turned once only.

To test if a steak is cooked, the meat should be put on a plate and tested with a finger pressure — it should spring back.

Degrees of cooking

- Rare — *au bleu* — very red.
- Underdone — *saigrant* — red centre.
- Just done — *à point* — just cooked.
- Well done — *bien cuit* — well cooked.

Offal

The edible parts taken from the inside of the animal's carcass, offal is an inexpensive form of protein and iron. As the majority of offal has a short shelf-life when it is fresh, care is needed to ensure that it is purchased and used when perfectly fresh. Much of the offal on sale in the UK is imported in a deep frozen state to ensure its freshness and good quality.

Liver and kidney contain protein, iron, and vitamins A and B.

Type	Origin	Characteristics	Method of use
Kidney	Ox	Dark, strong, tough texture.	Soups. Stews. Braised.
	Pig	Strong flavour, flat shape	Sautéd. Braised.
	Lamb/calf	Light delicate flavour.	Fried. Grilled.
Liver	Ox	Large size. Strong. Tough.	Braised.
	Pig	Strong flavour.	Pâté.
	Lamb	Mild flavour. Fine texture.	Fried. Grilled.
	Calf	Distinctive flavour. Soft.	Fried. Grilled
Tongue	Ox	Coarse texture. Tough.	Salted, boiled.
	Lamb	Small size. Tender texture.	Boiled.
Tripe	Ox	Honeycomb — wrinkled, second part of stomach Smooth — first part of stomach.	Boiled. Braised. Creamed. Boiled. Braised.

Type	Origin	Characteristics	Method of use
Sweet breads	Lamb and calf	Heartbread — round, best quality. Throatbread — long, even shape.	Fried. Creamed Fried. Braised
Heart	Ox	Dark colour. Tough texture.	Braised, sliced for service.
	Lamb/calf	Lighter colour. Tender, compact.	Braised, stuffed.
Tail	Ox	Even-sized bones. Dark flesh.	Stewed. Soups. Braised.
Head	Sheep/calf	Even layer of flesh.	Stock. Broths.

Pork

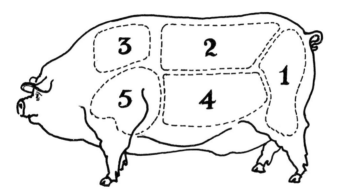

Pork cuts

Cuts	Uses	Service	Accompaniments
1. *Leg*	Roast	Sliced on a flat dish with roast potatoes.	Roast gravy. Apple sauce.
2. *Loin*	Chops	In shallow dish with apple rings.	Sauté potatoes. Gravy.
3. *Spare rib*	Roast	Sliced on silver flat with thickened gravy.	Sage and onion stuffing.
	Pies	Cold with salads.	Mayonnaise.
4. *Belly*	Fried	In shallow dish.	Jacket potatoes. Tomatoes.
5. *Shoulder*	Sausages	In shallow dish with bacon rashers.	Sauté potatoes. Tomatoes.

Quality points

- Smooth skin
- Pink fine flesh
- White smooth fat

Storage

- Kept very carefully, away from other meats, for a short length of time at 1°C in a refrigerator.

Nutritional value

Originating mainly from Britain and Denmark, pork contains protein, fat, and vitamin B.

Ham

This is produced when the hind leg of a porker pig is soaked in brine and then smoked. The different woods used to produce the smoke will alter the flavour of the ham.

Ham is cooked either by boiling in water, allowing 25 minutes to every 500g and 25 minutes over, or by placing in a steamer and allowing it to cook slowly in the moist heat. If it is to be served hot, the joint should be skinned and set to rest for 20 minutes before carving. In this case, a parsley sauce is usually served with the slices of ham. If it is to be used when cold, the joint should be skinned while hot and then placed in a mould to enable it to keep its moisture and shape while cooling down as rapidly as possible. A weight is placed on top of the mould to press the ham into a compact joint. When firm and cold it may be sliced thinly to be served with salads, or used for sandwiches.

Safety

The following points must be remembered when dealing with pork or pork products:
- Pork must be absolutely fresh and very well cooked to avoid trichinosis, which is caused by worms found in raw pork.
- If it is to be roasted, the pork joint must be cooked for 30 minutes per 500g.
- Foods containing pork must be stored for the minimum time possible and kept just above freezing point until service time. Items such as pork pies and sausage rolls must be kept in a chilled cabinet until ready to be eaten; they must never be placed on a counter where their internal temperature can rise.
- Foods made up from pork, and cooked to be eaten when hot,

must be thoroughly cooked and kept hot for the minimum possible length of time. Keeping foods, such as sausages and pork burgers, hot will allow the bacteria in such foods to multiply — unless they are kept *very* hot. This excess heat will spoil the product, so it is necessary to cook these items in small batches as demand dictates — eliminating the need to keep them hot.

- Sausages are manufactured from pork meat scraps, pork fat, cereal products, seasonings and preservatives. They should be very well cooked, never eaten raw, or browned outside and left raw in the centre. Once thawed they must be cooked thoroughly; if served cold they should be cooled rapidly and kept cold and covered until ready to be consumed.

Convenience pork products

There are many varieties of pork products because of the dangers of fresh pork:

Frozen
- Sausages — made from pork, pork and beef, and pork and herbs.
  — sausage meat, and sausage rolls, which are ready to bake.
- Burgers — diced pork and seasonings flattened into an oval shape.

Canned
- Chopped ham and pork — pork luncheon meat and stuffed pork roll.
- Shoulder of ham — pressed ham.
- Pork and ham pastes and spreads for sandwiches.

Fresh baked
- Pork pies and sausage rolls.

Lamb

Quality points

- Smooth skin
- Lean, dark red meat
- White brittle fat

Storage

- Hung in refrigerator at $1°C$ or on clean trays.

Nutritional value

Coming from England, Wales, New Zealand and Australia, lamb contains protein, fat, and vitamin B.

Cuts of lamb

Cut	Use	Service	Accompaniments
1. *Scrag end*	Broth	In soup bowl.	Bread roll
2. *Middle neck*	Braised	In shallow dish on a silver flat.	Turned root vegetables, and chopped parsley
3. *Best end*	Roast — crown	On flat dish with forcemeat stuffing.	Roast gravy
	Cutlets, fried	With tomatoes and mushrooms on flat dish.	Mint jelly or sauce
4. *Loin*	Roast	On flat dish with château potatoes.	Roast gravy, mint sauce and glazed root vegetables
	Loin chops, fried	On silver flat with watercress.	Straw potatoes, tomatoes and mushrooms
	Saddle, roast	On large flat dish.	Roast potatoes and gravy
5. *Leg*	Roast	Sliced onto flat dish with roast potatoes.	Roast gravy and mint sauce
	Chump chop	On silver flat with watercress.	Mint jelly and glazed root vegetables
6. *Breast*	Roast	Sliced onto shallow dish with forcemeat stuffing.	Thickened gravy and roast potatoes

Cut	Use	Service	Accompaniments
7. *Shoulder*	Roast	Sliced onto flat dish with turned root vegetables.	Roast potatoes, mint sauce and roast gravy
	Pies	Pie dish cleaned and placed onto plate with pie frill.	Thickened gravy

Definitions

- **Boiled leg of mutton:** Allow 25 minutes per 500g and 25 minutes over. This is normally served with boiled vegetables and some of the liquor is served separately. Caper sauce is usually served to accompany this traditional English dish.
- **Chump chop:** Cut from the area between the loin and the leg of lamb joint. It is cut to 2.5cm thickness and is oval in shape. It is very lean and the most popular type of lamb chop.
- **Cutlet:** Cut from the best end joint and smaller than a loin chop. Cutlets are 1.5cm thick and a long thin shape, with a small quantity of lean meat. They are trimmed before being cooked.
- **Lamb:** Most sheep are slaughtered when they are between three and twelve months old; this produces a carcass of lamb which may be sold either fresh or deep frozen as a whole or half carcass. It may be butchered into joints when it is thawed out later.
- **Loin chop:** Cut from the loin of lamb. Not very large in portion size and therefore often served with other meat items or with two or three loin chops to make an acceptable portion. It is sometimes possible to purchase double loin chops, which are cut from the saddle to make a larger portion.
- **Mutton:** Term given to a sheep carcass that is more than one year old. Mutton takes longer to cook than lamb and so is normally cooked using moist slow methods.
- **Mutton pies:** These are made of the cheaper cuts from the carcass and are made to many different regional recipes. The slow cooking of the diced or minced mutton is essential.
- **Roast leg of mutton:** Allow 25 minutes per 500g and 25 minutes over. This is served with roast gravy and either a white onion sauce or redcurrant jelly as an accompaniment.
- **Saddle:** The name given to a pair of loins. Kept whole without splitting down the centre backbone. Roasted as one large joint, average weight 5.5kg. Only used for large functions.
- **Stewed or braised mutton:** Diced or small cuts of mutton may be braised or stewed in many different dishes, such as Haricot Mutton. The slow moist methods make very successful dishes.

Poultry

Chicken is an easily digested meat with a high protein, low fat content. Fresh poultry is available throughout the year. Frozen poultry is of excellent quality and is also readily available.

Types	Sizes	Uses
Chicken	1.5–2kg	Roast. Sauté.
Boiling fowl	2–2.5kg	Soup. Fricassée.
Capon	2.5–3kg	Roast.
Spring chicken	1–1.5kg	Grill. Roast.
Poussin	1 per portion	Grill. Roast.
Turkey	5kg upwards	Roast.
Duck	2–3kg	Roast. Braise.

Giblets

- The edible parts from the inside of the bird, consisting of the neck, heart, and liver.
- Used for making gravy, stock, and soups. The livers are used for making pâté, omelet fillings, and some savouries.

Quality

Fresh
- The tip of the breastbone should be soft and pliable.
- The feet should be smooth and the scales small and flat.
- The skin should be unbroken and white.
- The breast should be plump and have little fat.

Frozen
- The wrapping should be clean and unbroken.
- The poultry should be labelled with weight and package date.
- The giblets should be in a small bag inside the body cavity.
- There should be no chalky white areas or lumps of ice.

Care when using frozen poultry

All frozen poultry must be fully thawed before being cooked. The best way is to allow it to thaw out in the refrigerator on a clean tray, where it will be kept cool whilst defrosting. If short of time, a microwave may be used to defrost the poultry safely. The poultry must, however, be used as soon as it has been thawed if this method is used, as the microwave oven will cause the flesh to become slightly warm and encourage bacteria growth.

For example, study the following:

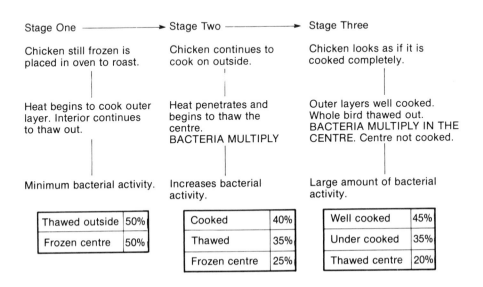

Turkey

- The largest turkey can weigh up to 20kg; these large birds need long slow cooking.
- There is approximately 50 per cent white meat from the breast and wings and 50 per cent dark meat from the rest of the bird.
- It may be a dry meat unless well basted while being roasted and cooked slowly.

Duck

- A rich dark meat with more fat present than in other types of poultry.
- Needs to be cooked slowly and with care so that the flesh does not fall from the bones.
- The most famous breed is Aylesbury duck.
- Should be cooked in a way that will eliminate any excess fat.
- Ducklings are the young birds that are best roasted; they serve 2 persons.

Convenience Poultry Items

	Type	Characteristics	Menu uses
Frozen	Whole birds	Prepared and trimmed.	Sauté. Fricassée. Roast.
	Butter basted	Prepared and butter injected. Needs no basting.	Roast.
	Chicken portions	One-portion sized pieces on the bone. Trimmed.	Grilled. Fried. Cooked in microwave.
	Boneless breasts	Trimmed boneless. All white meat.	Chicken dishes that require minimum cooking time.
	Turkey/chicken roasts	Prepared, formed, boneless flesh in roll shape.	Roast. Served cold for rolls, sandwiches, buffets.
	Drumsticks	The legs trimmed.	Devilled or roast. Served hot or cold.
Breaded	Fingers	Chicken flesh formed into small bar-shaped pieces.	Deep-fried. Bar snacks. School meals. Buffets.
	Nuggets	Flesh formed to small oval shapes.	Deep fried. Fast food. Bar snacks.
	Turkey/chicken steaks	Flesh formed into round cakes, thin.	Children's meals. Fast food.
	Pies	Individual sized, short-crust pastry.	Children's meals. Bar snacks. Fast food.
Canned	Pie-filling	Diced flesh in velouté sauce.	Welfare and industrial catering.
	Cooked chicken roll	Cooked lean flesh, no fat or waste. White meat.	Sliced for buffets, sandwiches and rolls.
	Chicken pâté	Finely ground, well seasoned chicken mix.	Hors d'oeuvres. Filled rolls and sandwiches.
	Chicken paste	Smooth, well seasoned paste.	Sandwiches. Welfare units. School meals.

Poultry-based Dishes

Dish	Method summary	Service
Roast chicken *Poulet rôti*	Roast 20 minutes per 500g and 20 minutes extra, in a moderate oven.	Roast gravy. Game chips. Watercress.
Roast stuffed chicken *Poulet à l'Anglaise*	Chicken with parsley and thyme forcemeat. Roast as above, allowing time for forcemeat to cook through.	Roast gravy. Game chips. Watercress. Stuffing sliced with each portion.
Roast stuffed duck *Canard rôti à l'Anglaise*	Duck with sage and onion forcemeat. Roast 25 minutes per 500g and 25 minutes extra in a moderate oven.	Roast gravy. Slices of stuffing with each portion. Hot apple sauce. Watercress
Roast turkey *Dinde rôti*	Turkey with chestnut and sausage stuffing placed in neck end. Parsley and thyme forcemeat inside carcass. Roast 30 minutes per 500g and 30 minutes extra in moderate oven.	Roast gravy. Slices of both types of stuffing per portion. Bread sauce served separately. Cranberry sauce. Bacon rolls.
Sauté chicken *Poulet roti*	Cut to joints and sauté gently to ensure thoroughly cooked. Never coated with sauce until served.	Joints coated with the appropriate sauce — chasseur, demi-glace. Placed in shallow dish, sprinkled with parsley.
Grilled chicken *Poulet grillé*	Trimmed halved/quartered pieces of chicken seasoned, brushed with oil, gently grilled — 20 minutes per side until well cooked.	Portions placed on flat dish garnished with watercress. A sharp sauce served separately.
Deep-fried chicken. *Poulet faire frire*	Small-sized pieces of chicken are floured, egg and breadcrumbed, and deep fried on medium heat, until cooked through.	Portions are well drained and served either hot or cold with tossed green salad and chipped potatoes.

Dish	Method summary	Service
Boiled chicken and rice *Poulet poché au riz*	Boiled chicken, portioned as cooked.	Chicken coated with chicken velouté sauce, finished with cream, and served on a bed of rice.
Chicken cutlets *Côtelettes de volaille*	Finely diced cooked chicken mixed with panada velouté. Mixture formed to cutlet shape, floured, egg and breadcrumbed.	Carefully fried until golden brown and crisp. Served on flat dish with watercress. Strong flavoured sauce offered separately — Madeira or mushroom.
Fricassée of chicken *Fricassée de volaille*	Small-sized pieces of chicken sautéed without colouring. A velouté sauce finished with cream.	Chicken placed in shallow dish, coated with well seasoned sauce. Sprinkled with chopped parsley.
Chicken casserole *Poulet en casserole*	Whole chicken or portions are placed on bed of root vegetables with minimum quantity of stock. Cooked in moderate oven.	Chicken placed in clean dish, coated with demi-glace sauce. Garnished with glazed root vegetables and onions.
Curried chicken *Currie de poulet*	Chicken pieces browned in pan, curry sauce added and cooked gently until chicken tender.	Served on a bed of boiled rice in a shallow dish. Curry accompaniments offered.

Unit 6 Assessment Activities

1. (a) Visit a fish market or large fishmongers and identify the fish presented for sale.
   (b) Describe at least two ways of preparing and cooking each of the fish that you have identified.

2. (a) Describe ways of creating acceptable dishes using cooked flaked white fish.
   (b) Indicate how these dishes should be garnished and presented to the customer to maximise sales.

3. (a) Describe the differences between bacon and pork.
   (b) List ways that may be used to cook cheaper cuts of bacon.
   (c) Suggest safety points to be included on a staff-training poster indicating the uses of pork, pork products, and poultry.

4. (a) Describe the method used to roast a joint of meat.
   (b) List the joints of beef, lamb and pork that may be cooked successfully using the roasting method.
   (c) Suggest suitable accompaniments for these named joints.

5. (a) Find out the costs of the seven joints that are obtainable from a side of lamb.
   (b) Name and describe two recipes for each of these seven joints, giving a costing for these recipes.

Unit 7:

Nutritional Aspects and Food

Rechauffé Cookery

Rechauffé cookery is any food that has been cooked, allowed to cool and is then re-heated. The original food may be made into an entirely different dish.

Rules for preparation

- The food must be absolutely fresh.
- Immediately the service is over, any remaining food should be cooled rapidly, placed in clean containers and put into the refrigerator.
- Divide the food up finely — mince, flake, chop, slice or mash — to allow the heat to penetrate quickly.
- Reheat the foods quickly and thoroughly but do not re-cook the foods as this will harden the protein fibres and make the food indigestible.
- Additional foods used for flavouring, and to add bulk to the dish, need to be pre-cooked and absolutely fresh.
- Additional moisture is usually required, often in the form of a sauce. This will help to supply flavour and colour.
- Seasoning is necessary as re-heated foods lose much of their original flavour.
- Foods are often protected from the direct heat to prevent re-cooking.

Methods of protection	*Flavourings*
• Coating in egg and breadcrumbs	• Salt, pepper, mustard
• Coating with potato — shepherds pie	• Onion, tomato purée
• Dipping in batter — fritters	• Garlic, curry powder
• Sealed in pastry — pasties	• Beef extract, mushrooms
	• Mixed herbs, Worcester sauce

Hints for service

- Rechauffé dishes should be served as soon as possible after cooking. They should be very hot.
- Prepare in individual dishes so that presentation is easy and attractive.
- Plan a variety of textures by using crisp toast, fried coatings, or raw salad vegetables as accompaniments.
- Use a variety of colour in the garnish by using parsley, watercress, tomato, celery, mushrooms, lemon, etc. as appropriate.
- Always use the quickest form of heat. The microwave is very

useful for many rechauffé dishes, it will reheat very quickly from the centre of the food to the outside, so eliminating a cold centre.
- Bacterial activity must be kept to a minimum; so all foods must be kept very cold or very hot and served immediately.

Food Preservation

The preservation of foods may be achieved by any of the following methods:

Removing moisture
- Restricting the amount of water available for any reactions to take place. This includes the processes known as: drying; dehydrating; salting; sugaring.

Making the food cold
- Slowing down or immobilizing the action of any harmful bacteria that may be present in the food by either chilling, or freezing the foods.

Applying heat
- Placing the foods in sealed containers and then applying a high temperature for sufficient length of time to destroy the bacteria in the foods. This includes the processes known as canning and bottling.

Making conditions acid
- Placing the prepared foods in vinegar, as in the process known as pickling.

Adding chemicals
- Adding chemical preservatives, such as nitrate to cooked meats and sausages.

The effect of preservation upon nutrients

By the time they are eaten, preserved products have probably suffered no more than their fresh equivalents, which have lost nutrients during their transportation and cooking. It must be remembered that only very fresh foods may be successfully preserved, and only good quality products are accepted by the preservation companies.

Protein: Little obvious effect is found.

Fats: Little effect, except for a tendency to go rancid in quick freezing if not stored at a very low temperature.

Carbohydrate: After quick freezing, sugar and starch become more easily digested due to oxidation reactions.

Vitamins: Vitamins B and C are lost by about 25 per cent on average. Vitamin D is lost during dehydration. But Vitamin A suffers little loss.

Using Left-over Foods for Rechauffé Dishes

Food left-over	Dishes
Roast beef	Miroton of beef. Shepherd's Pie. Minced beef.
Braised steaks	Diced and made into meat and potato pie.
Lamb chops	Curried lamb chops.
Boiled mutton	Moussaka. Mutton pies.
Roast pork	Minced and used in rissoles, Kromeski.
Boiled ham	Omelet filling. Veal and ham pie. Spaghetti Milanaise.
Chicken liver	Chicken liver omelet. Pâté.
Sauté kidney	Kidney omelet. Kidney soup.
Boiled chicken	Chicken á la king. Chicken cutlets.
Sauté chicken	Curried chicken.
Poached white fish	Fish pie. Fish cakes. Fish pasties.
Poached smoked fish	Kedgeree. Fish cakes. Fish pies.
Poached eggs	Placed in tartlets with cheese sauce, glazed.
Hard-boiled eggs	Scotch eggs. Egg croquettes. Egg chimay.
Cheese — grated	Quiche Lorraine. Mornay sauce. Omelets.
Baked jacket potatoes	Sauté potatoes. Stuffed in jackets. Potato salad.
Boiled potatoes	Potato croquettes. Potatoes au gratin.
Boiled mixed vegetables	Vegetable salads. Garnish for rice dishes.
Boiled cabbage	Bubble and squeak. Braised cabbage.
Boiled onions	Stuffed braised onions.
Boiled celery	Braised celery.
Boiled cauliflower	Cauliflower mornay. Florets fried in batter.
Mushrooms	Mushroom sauce. Deep fried in batter.
Boiled rice	Rice salad. Placed in mixed vegetable soups.
Boiled spaghetti	Pasta and vegetable salad. Minestrone soup.
Boiled macaroni	Macaroni au gratin.

Preservation Methods

Type	Method	Foods	Use
Sterilization Canning	The food is placed into sealed containers so that further bacteria cannot enter. The container is heated to destroy the bacteria which are present.	Veg. — water/sauce	Reheat
		Fruit — solid pack	Pies, puddings.
		Fruit — syrup	Flans, gâteaux
		Fish — oil/sauce	Hors d'oeuvres
		Meat — ham in juice	Sliced, salads
		— steak in gravy	Meat pies
		Milk — evaporated	Milk puddings
		— condensed	
Quick freezing	The temperature of the product is reduced as rapidly as possible to $-18°C$ at its centre. The process prevents bacterial activity while the product is frozen.	Veg — free flow	Cook from frozen
		Fruit — free flow	Thaw and use
		Fish — pre-prepared	Thaw before use
		Fish fillets, whole	Thaw before use
		Meat — butchered	Thaw before use
		Meat pre-prepared	Thaw before use
		Bakery — breads — pastry items	Thaw slowly then use at once
Pickling	The foods are soaked in acid, usually a vinegar, where the acidity is too high to allow the growth of bacteria.	Onions, olives gherkins, red cabbage, beetroot, mint sauce, mixed pickled veg., chutney	All ready to use straight from the jar in which they are preserved
Curing	The availability of water for the bacteria is reduced by soaking the food in a brine solution	Beef — silverside	Boiled
		— brisket	Boiled, pressed
		Bacon — may be smoked after curing in brine	Rashers grilled or fried
		Pork — makes ham	Ham used sliced

Preservation Methods (*Continued*)

Type	Method	Foods	Use
Roller or spray dried	The food products are passed over or sprayed onto heated drum/rollers. Scraped off when dry.	Potato powder	Creamed potato dishes
		Instant coffee	Individual cups
		Milk powder	Substitute for fresh milk
		Egg powder	Replaces egg in bakery items
Dehydration	The product is dried in hot air at a reduced air-pressure to speed up the process, and reduce the risk of cooking the product itself.	Soup mixes and sauce mixes	Blend with water, simmer 20 minutes
		Pulses — peas, beans and lentils Cereals, e.g. pearl barley	Soak for 24 hours, then cook until tender
		Fruits — apricots prunes, apples.	Use as required.
Pre-blanched dehydrated	The products are first blanched, then dehydrated.	Currants, sultanas and raisins	In bakery items
		Meats — minced, sliced	Commercially added to dehydrated meals
Accelerated freeze dried	The product is first frozen, then passed through a vacuum. The sudden loss of atmospheric pressure turns the ice to steam, thereby leaving the food in a porous dehydrated condition.	Pieces of meat and fish	Soak for 20 minutes then use as required
		Diced vegetables	Soups, sauces and pies
		Soft fruits	Puddings and pies

134

Convenience Foods

Convenience foods are prepared or pre-prepared products that require the minimum time to reconstitute and use. They are normally used in conjunction with traditional methods of food preparation to supplement fresh ingredients. All convenience foods have a limited shelf-life and generally it is not economical to purchase more than can be used over a reasonable period of time. Once unsealed, packets must be used within a few days; therefore most items are packaged in small quantities, for example, dehydrated soup mixes that make 4 litres of soup. Canned foods will keep for a considerable length of time as long as they are unopened; as soon as they have been unsealed they must be used within 24 hours.

Convenience Products

Foods	Dehydrated	Frozen-raw	Frozen-cooked	Canned	Bottled
Soups	X			X	
Sauces	X			X	X
Stocks	X				
Potatoes	X	X	X	X	
Pulses	X			X	
Root veg	X	X		X	
Salads				X	X
Meats		X	X	X	
Fish		X	X	X	
Meat/pastry		X	X		
Pastry	X	X	X		
Ice cream	X	X			
Fruit	X	X		X	X

Overleaf is an example of a basic menu which uses convenience products.

A simple menu using convenience foods

Mixed Vegetable Soup (Dehydrated soup mix.)

Fillet of Plaice	(Frozen breadcrumbed.)
Chicken Pie	(Canned pie filling; dehydrated pastry mix.)

Chipped Potatoes	(Frozen — pre-blanched.)
Mixed Vegetables	(Frozen mixed.)

Chocolate Gâteau	(Dehydrated sponge mix.)
Fruit Salad	(Canned in syrup.)

Coffee (Instant granules and UHT cream.)

The Effect of Heat Upon Foods

Foods are cooked to make them more palatable, more easily digested, more attractive and safer, as harmful bacteria are destroyed.

Meat
- The protein coagulates, making the meat tough if overcooked.
- Elastin in muscle fibre shrinks.
- Collagen turns to gelatine, making fibres tender.
- The red colour of lean meats turns brown.
- The fat melts and turns liquid; in dry heat it turns brown.
- The meat juices dissolve out and the meat therefore shrinks.

Fish
- The protein coagulates; there is a little shrinkage.
- The extractives dissolve out, causing loss of flavour and shape.

Milk
- The protein coagulates and a skin forms on the surface.
- The lactose caramelizes during slow cooking, making it burn easily.
- Milk fats soften, making warm milk easier to digest.
- The bacteria are destroyed during pasteurization.

Eggs
- The protein coagulates — the white at 60°C and the yolk at 65°C.
- The yolk of egg becomes powdery and dry if over-heated.
- Over-cooking causes the proteins to shrink.
- When eggs are mixed with liquids and heated shrinkage occurs, causing the mixture to curdle and separate.
- Dry heat causes carbonization, therefore egg is used for glazing.

136

Cheese
- The protein coagulates and shrinks.
- Over-cooking makes the protein hard and indigestible.
- Dry heat causes carbonization, therefore cheese is used for gratinating dishes.
- Long cooking causes stringiness of the cheese.

Cereals
- Cooking is essential for their digestion by humans.
- The starch grains burst and gelatinize. Liquids are absorbed.
- Dry heat causes dextrinization, carbonization and colour change; for example, baked products colour and bread turns to toast.

Vegetables
- The cellulose cell walls soften and lose shape if overcooked.
- The starch in potatoes gelatinizes and becomes powdery.
- The starch becomes more easily digested.
- Vitamin C and mineral salts are lost in the cooking liquid.
- Vitamin C is lost when finely shredded, chopped or grated.

Fruit
- The cellulose cell walls soften.
- Vitamin C content is lost.
- Mineral salts and fructose are lost in the cooking liquid.
- Fruits soften and lose shape if overcooked.

Sugar
- Sugar becomes soluble as it warms.
- Sugar will caramelize as the heat is increased, changing colour.
- Increased heat causes the sugar to burn to carbon.

Bread dough
- The steam causes the dough to rise following the expansion of the carbon dioxide.
- Yeast activity increases, it is destroyed at $55°C$.
- The starch grains swell and gelatinize.
- Gluten coagulates at $70°C$, giving the bread its final shape.
- Water and carbon dioxide are driven off during baking.
- Starch dextrinizes and the sugar caramelizes, giving colour change.

Puff paste
- The moisture in the dough is converted to steam, which causes the pastry layers to rise.
- The fat is melted and absorbed into the pastry.
- The starch grains swell and burst.
- The gluten coagulates, giving the pastry its final shape.

Shortcrust pastry
- Vapour is formed and driven off by the heat between the particles of fat.
- The particles of fat are forced apart to create a short texture.

Sponge mixture
- The heat expands the air, which is trapped in the egg albumen.
- The gluten in the flour coagulates.
- The expansion of the air causes the sponge to rise. The air is retained when the sponge sets and is cooled.

Meringues
- The heat solidifies the aerated structure of the meringue.
- The egg albumen coagulates.

Nutrition

A balanced diet

This will be obtained by using the variety of foods needed to keep an individual in a healthy and fit state. The recommended minimum basic requirements for an adult per day are:

Milk — 500 ml.
Meat or fish — 1 serving.
Cheese or eggs — 1 serving.
Fresh vegetables — 2 servings.
Fresh fruit — 2 servings.
Cereals, unrefined.
Bread, wholemeal.
Fats, fortified margarine.
Liquids — 1.5 litres.

- Meals may be created to include any variety of foods that will suit the customer but care should always be taken to consider the overall nutritional content.
- Concern is frequently expressed about the quantity of fibre taken in the diet. Foods with a high fibre content should be included in the daily intake of food.
- The level of animal fat consumed is considered by some people to have a bearing on good health; it is therefore worth looking at the animal fat intake and if possible substituting less harmful vegetable fats, such as replacing butter with a vegetable-based margarine, or lard with vegetable oil.
- Two small, or even three small, meals per 24 hours are easier for the body to utilize than one large meal.

Digestion

This is the process by which foods are broken down and converted into a form that the body can assimilate:

Stage 1	Stage 2	Stage 3
MOUTH	STOMACH	INTESTINE
Teeth — break up food fibre Saliva — moistens food and begins digestion of starch Tongue — pushes food particles into oesophagus	Walls — contract, squeeze, churn contents Pepsin — digests protein Rennin — digests milk Gastric juices — digest starch	Bile — neutralizes mild irritants and emulsifies fats Pancreatic juices — digestion of protein, fats converted to fatty acids, starch converted to sugars
Food broken up and chewed by teeth	Food churned round and liquidized	Digestion complete. Liver stores glucose, iron and Vitamin B

Stage 4	Stage 5
Food is absorbed into bloodstream	Waste products passed to bladder and rectum

Foods Required by the Body

Nutrient	Food in which found	Function of nutrient
Animal protein	Meat, fish, eggs, dairy produce	Builds the body and repairs tissues
Vegetable protein	Pulses, nuts, cereals	Heat and energy
Carbohydrate — starch, sugar	Bread, cakes, pulses, potatoes, milk, beer, roots, fruits, honey	Heat and energy Helps use fats
Animal fat	Butter, lard, dripping, suet	Heat and energy, excess stored away
Vegetable fat	Margarine, vegetable oils	
Calcium	Dairy produce, tinned salmon, milk, bread, green vegetables	Strengthens teeth and bones Works with Vitamin D
Phosphorus	Bread, eggs, fish, cheese, liver, kidney	Strengthens bones and nerves

Nutrient	Food in which found	Function of nutrient
Iron	Lean meat, offal, egg, fish, green vegetables, wholemeal flour	Assists red blood corpuscles
Fibre (roughage)	Wholemeal bread, oatmeal, fruit, unrefined cereals, vegetables	Prevents constipation
Vitamin A (destroyed by sunlight, heat or excessive storage)	Eggs, milk, green vegetables, apricots, fish, carrots, tomatoes, margarine	Eyes in good order Promotes growth and resists disease
Vitamin B_1 — thiamine (water soluble)	Yeast, offal, pork, eggs, pulses, cereals, green vegetables, bacon	Nervous system kept in good order
Vitamin B_2 — riboflavin (water soluble, destroyed by heat and sunlight)	Yeast, wholemeal flour, offal, milk, cheese, eggs, fish, green vegetables, meat	Growth of young healthy skin
Vitamin C (water soluble)	Citrus fruits, soft fruits, green vegetables, peas, beans, parsley, blackcurrants	Resists infection, promotes general good health
Vitamin D (fat soluble)	Fish, milk, eggs, butter, margarine, the action of sunlight upon the skin	Works with calcium

Flavourings

Herbs, spices, and condiments have little food value in themselves, but they are used extensively to enhance and bring out the maximum flavour of foods.

The difference between a herb and a spice is that herbs are dried leaves of culinary plants, while true spices are the highly flavoured products of various types of plants; they may be prepared from the roots, bark, fruit, stem or berry of the plant.

Condiments

Block salt — For kitchen use and for adding to foods while cooking.

Table salt — Free-flowing; used in salt cellars for seasoning foods at the table.

Iodised salt — Salt with potassium iodine added; it has a short shelf-life and is used in salt cellars.

Sea salt — Pungent, coarse texture; used in salt mills for additional seasoning at the table.

White pepper — Used for flavouring light-coloured foods and dishes.

Black pepper — A hot pepper used in pepper mills and for seasoning meat dishes prior to service.

Cayenne pepper — Very pungent pepper, sparingly used; found in curry powder.

Paprika pepper — Pungent pepper used in Hungarian goulash, and as a colour garnish.

Tabasco sauce — A liquid manufactured from hot peppers; used to flavour sea foods.

Curry powder — Made from a mixture of ginger, cayenne, turmeric, cinnamon, nutmeg, mace, clove, salt, coriander, and pepper. Used for curry sauces, mulligatawny soup, etc.

Worcester sauce — A mixture of spices made into a pungent sauce. Used for flavouring hot foods and sprinkling onto chilled tomato juice.

Mushroom ketchup — A liquid mushroom-flavoured dark sauce made from mushroom essence. Used to increase the flavour of meat-based dishes such as meat pies, puddings, and meat sauces.

Soy sauce — An oriental sauce manufactured from herbs and spices to produce a dark pungent sauce, sprinkled sparingly on foods.

Tomato ketchup — A thick sauce manufactured from tomatoes with spices and vinegar. Served as an additional accompaniment for hot snacks, such as fish and chips, and beef burgers.

H.P. sauce — A smooth brown sauce, pungent in flavour, made from spices, vegetables, and vinegar. Served as an additional accompaniment for hot snack foods, such as meat pies.

Fruity sauce — A smooth brown sauce, slightly sweet-tasting; used as an additional accompaniment for hot snack foods, such as fried sausage and chips.

Herbs

Herbs may be used fresh when available, but most dried herbs have a stronger flavour; if using dried herbs only half the quantity is required because the moisture content has been reduced. Herbs should be stored in airtight containers and care should be taken to purchase them in a quantity that permits a reasonably short storage life. Dried herbs will lose flavour and colour if stored for too long a time in a light, warm atmosphere.

Selected Herbs

Type	Uses
Basil	Tomato-based dishes, poultry, veal, liver, kidneys, fish, shellfish.
Bayleaf	Bouquet garni, dried mixed herbs, white fish.
Chervil	In 'fines herbes' mixture for flavouring, soups, egg dishes, salads, vegetable dishes.
Dill — seeds	Aids digestion of cabbage, coleslaw, sauerkraut, chutneys, root vegetables.
— leaves	Cream cheese, omelets, salads, lamb, veal, chicken, fish dishes, rice, vegetables.
Fennel — seeds	Aids digestion of starchy foods, such as bread, pastries, and leaf vegetables.
— leaves	Fish dishes, baked fish, green salad, potatoes.
Mint	Potatoes and legume vegetables, lamb dishes.
Parsley	Garnishes, sauces, salads, poultry and fish dishes.
Rosemary	Aids digestion of rich foods; complements meats.
Sage	Helps to digest rich foods, pork, duck, in stuffings.
Sorrel	Salads, cooked as a vegetable, soups, sauces.
Tarragon	Poultry, game, offal, salads.
Thyme	Soups, stews, with parsley in stuffings, bouquet-garni, mixed herbs.

Examples of some common herbs:
Top row (left to right) — rosemary, basil, marjoram, tarragon.
Bottom row (left to right) — sage, thyme, parsley, bay.

Spices

Spices come from plants that have a pungent flavour; when the spice is extracted and dried it is even stronger in flavour. The spices may be extracted from various parts of the plants, the roots, bark, seed, or pod, and are sold ground or whole. They must be stored in airtight jars as they become less pungent with age.

Useful spice mixes include the following:

Pickling spice — allspice, black peppercorns, mustard seed, fennel seed, dill seed, chillies, cinnamon, bay leaves.
Indian curry — coriander, cumin, turmeric, ginger, chilli, cinnamon, cloves, mustard, black pepper.
Mixed spice — coriander, cinnamon, allspice, nutmeg, ginger, cloves.

Selected spices

Type	Part	Uses
Allspice	Berries	Flavours cakes, puddings, stewed fruit.
Chilli	Fruit	Pungent flavour in spicy casseroles, rice dishes.
Cinnamon	Bark	Mulled wine, casseroles, apple dishes, cakes.
Cloves	Buds	Pickles, puddings, stewed and baked fruits.
Coriander	Seeds	Fish and poultry, fruit cakes, pastries.
Cumin	Seeds	Hot pungent seed used in meat and rice dishes.
Ginger	Root	Fruit cakes, biscuits, pickles, sauces, puddings.
Nutmeg	Kernel	Egg-based sweets, fruit cakes, puddings, sauces.
Turmeric	Root	Flavouring pickles and colouring kedgeree, curry, etc.
Vanilla	Pod/bean	Custards, ices, sauces, cakes, puddings.

Ginger

Cloves

Nutmeg

Cinnamon

Vanilla

144

Food additives

The addition of chemical substances to food is controlled by the Food and Drugs Act (1955) and only extremely small quantities are permitted.

Monosodium glutamate is a widely used chemical food additive that intensifies the natural food flavour by stimulating the gastric juices when the food is placed in the mouth. It is a white crystalline soluble substance, used in many manufactured meat products such as pies, pasties, burgers, and sausages.

Food Colours

Yellow	Saffron	Very expensive colouring agent used to colour boiled rice and other items deep yellow.
	Turmeric	Fine powder prepared form the stem of the plant. Used for curry powder, mustard, and pickles.
	Annato	The seeds of the plant are used to produce a bright yellow agent, used for colouring cheese red, and some pickles and sauces.
Green	Chlorophyll	A natural green colour taken from the leaves of spinach and sorrel by means of a solvent. Used to colour pasta.
Red	Cochineal	Obtained from a species of Central American insect. Used for tinting confectionery goods.
Blue	Indigo	Deep blue colour obtained from the indigo plant. Used in minute quantities to counteract the yellowish effect in white icings.
Mauve	Cochineal and indigo	A mauve colour may be created by blending these two agents together. Used for icings and artificial violets.
Brown	Caramel	Obtained by heating sugar to 174°C then dissolving the caramel to obtain the colour. Used in meat sauces and casseroles.
Dark brown	Blackjack	Obtained by heating sugar to 220°C, when a bitter dark caramel is obtained. Care is needed to ensure that the bitter flavour is not transferred, by using blackjack sparingly in gravies and meat glazes.

E numbers

Giving a number, prefixed by the letter E (standing for European), to food additives is the method used to code safe additives within the European Economic Community. All foods manufactured and packaged for sale now have to include the E number, or the actual name of the additive, in the list of ingredients in that particular product.

- Permitted colours E100–E180

  All kinds of foods now contain colour, but fresh meats, poultry, fish, fruits, vegetables, milk, tea, and coffee are all products that are *not* permitted to contain any colouring additives.

- Preservatives E200–E290

  These are used to prolong the 'safe period' for fresh made-up products, such as meat pies and sausages. They are also used to preserve products that are canned or bottled.

- Emulsifiers and stabilizers E322–E494

  Some of these may act as tenderizers for meat products. E450, a polyphosphate, is used to increase the volume of water that is retained in frozen poultry and meats.

- Sweeteners E420–E421

  These are used to increase the sweet taste in products.

- Solvents E422

  These are used to extract or dissolve foods so that they may be incorporated into other products.

- Mineral hydrocarbons E905–E907

  Used to prevent foods from drying out and to give foods a shiny appearance. Used in foods such as dried fruits, sugar, and confectionery.

- Modified starches E1400–E1442

  These are used in dairy products such as milk shakes.

Unit 7 Assessment Activities

1. (a) Describe the types of catering establishments that may use rechauffé cookery during their normal weekly trading.
   (b) Discuss how this method of utilising foods could be altered by the use of a microwave oven.

2. (a) Plan a series of menus suitable for a hotel table d'hôte menu, indicating how these menus could be prepared more economically by the use of convenience products.
   (b) State any difference that would be apparent with regard to: texture; colour; and taste.

3. Describe ways that a caterer may increase the protein content of meals by using dried pulses and TVP products.

4. (a) List dishes that are prepared with the use of herbs and spices.
   (b) Describe the predominant flavour of these dishes.

5. (a) Make a collection of convenience food packets and labels.
   (b) Analyse the ingredients used to produce these products and discuss your findings.

Unit 8:

Hygiene and Catering Premises

Principles of the Kitchen

The following aspects need to be considered when either planning a new food preparation area or redesigning an existing kitchen.

Goods inwards → Checked and stored → Issued and prepared → Served and sold

• Easy access • Unloading and parking areas.	• Secure area • Trained staff to check goods • Adequate store area	• Storekeeper to issue and record stores • Kitchen staff to prepare foods to their best advantage	• Foods garnished, packaged and sold in appetising manner • Clean appealing surroundings

Planning

- Location of water and fuel supplies and the drainage facilities must be investigated.
- Best use must be made of the area: it must be large enough to enable staff to carry out their work without accidents or crossed work flow lines.
- Floors must be non-slip, impervious, easily cleaned, and resistant to heat damage and stains from foods and cleaning agents.
- Walls and ceilings must be light-coloured, washable, and non-absorbent.

Lighting

- Use natural light wherever possible. Fluorescent lighting may be used to create as natural a colour as possible without causing any shadows or false colours on the food.
- There should be no dark unlit corners as these attract rodents.

Ventilation

- Always use natural ventilation as long as it will not be likely to create draughts.
- Fit removable mesh screens on windows to prevent flies and wasps from entering.
- Extractor fans and hoods, fitted above the main cooking areas to remove excess steam and cooking odours, will help to reduce unpleasant atmospheres. There must be adequate and quiet ventilation in all service areas.

Fuel

- Water: check the supply of drinking water. Determine the quantity of hot water that will be needed and then select the most suitable heating method.
- Cooking fuel: decide whether to have one type for the whole unit, or two types in case of overloading or emergencies. Compare the

running costs, storage, and delivery arrangements.
- Heating: measure the areas to be heated and check the availability of fuels and systems. Compare the costs and suitability of the systems.

Staffing

- The number of staff that will be in the unit at any one time will need to be estimated, as well as the total number of staff that will be employed.
- It will be necessary to plan the type and size of toilet and cloakroom facilities that will be supplied for the staff. A locker will be needed for each member of staff, and there must be a rest and dining room area with first-aid facilities. It will be necessary to provide hand-washing facilities in all parts of the unit.

Accident Prevention

Areas	Causes	Remedy
Floor	Wet/damp floor Food debris left on floor Brooms and mops lying in corner Boxes/cartons left by refuse sack	Clean tidy kitchen Cleaning rota Staff training
Light equipment	Knives and mandolins incorrectly used or handled Broken equipment. Equipment not stacked on shelves properly	Equipment cleaned and stacked properly Staff trained to use sharp implements
Heavy equipment	Oven doors left open Items placed on edges of ranges Incorrect lifting procedures	Heavy equipment used properly, and safely Staff training
Electrical equipment	Mis-use of equipment Wrong equipment attachments used Not disconnected from power before being cleaned. Broken plugs/flexes	Staff training Attachments coded for each machine Warning notices
Heat — dry	Solid top ranges left on Thermostats not working on hot plates Handles too hot	Staff training Equipment maintenance
Heat — wet	Incorrect use of steamers, boiling pans, water boilers, coffee machines	Staff training in uses/steam dangers

Areas	Causes	Remedy
Clothing	Cuffs, buttons, apron strings, caught in equipment Unsafe footwear	Adequate protective clothing Safe shoes, non-slip
Foods	Contaminated foods and foods that are incorrectly stored Foods and meals incorrectly carried	Staff awareness of causes of food poisoning Use of lifts/trolleys
Personnel	Staff running about Staff not concentrating upon the task to be completed Staff unaware of others	Staff training Staff supervision and motivation

Any accidents to staff or guests should be reported to the management immediately. A clear statement of events leading up to the accident must be written in the accident book, which should be kept in the manager's office. This report is essential even if the injured person does not appear to be badly hurt. An insurance claim may be filed at a later date and a detailed record will be required.

Washing-up

Washing up is the point at which a chain of infection is broken. The removal of bacteria, and their potential breeding grounds in the form of waste food, is the way to protect against an outbreak of food poisoning.

Points to be remembered
- Washing-up should be completed away from food preparation and storage areas.
- The sinks should not ever be used for any other purpose because of the risks of cross-infection.
- Because of the greasy nature of kitchen pans and equipment, these should be washed up in a separate area away from the cutlery, glassware, and tableware.
- A liquid detergent that has a bactericide added should be used to remove the grease and food debris, and destroy the bacteria.
- To ensure satisfactory results, correct temperatures must be maintained while washing and rinsing:

    Washing at $60°C \rightarrow$ *Rinsing* at $60°C \rightarrow$ *Sterilizing* at $82°C$

- After washing, pots and pans are best stored on racks in an inverted position.
- Crockery, glassware, and tableware should be stored in a position convenient to the washing-up area. Trolleys for the racks and trays are normally used to allow for easy and safe movement of such items without increased handling.
- All items should be stored in as dust-free an area as possible. Racks and trays that contain the clean items should be covered when not in use, using an additional tray, or a cloth, simply placed on top.

Washing-up by hand

Each piece of crockery is washed separately in the first sink that contains water at $60°C$ and a detergent. The washed crockery is then placed in a wire basket and lowered into the second sink, containing clear water held at $82°C$. The racks should be immersed in this very hot water for at least 2 minutes to ensure the destruction of the bacteria. The crockery should then remain in the racks to allow it to air-dry. Any further handling should be kept to a minimum to reduce the risk of further contamination by people's hands.

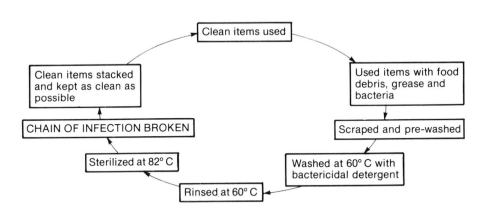

Washing-up by machine

It is possible to purchase and install a machine of any size, capacity and design to suit the volume of business; however, all machines follow the same sequence of basic cleaning — as shown below.

Process	Action	Result
1 Preparation	Scraping, soaking, pre-wash	Removal of all food debris and crumbs, grease, and sauces
2 Washing	Water at 60°C with a bactericide detergent Agitation with bristles to clean the items	Complete removal of all traces of food particles
3 Rinsing	Water sprayed onto racks Clear rinsing agent added	Complete removal of all greasy water
4 Sterilizing	Water sprayed onto racks at 82°C Sterilizing agent may be added	Complete destruction of all harmful bacteria
5 Drying	Racks removed and left to air-dry Minimum handling of items	Items are clean, and the rinsing agent added at stage 3 will ensure that they dry fast and spotless

Operator control machines: The time during which the washing, rinsing and sterilizing lasts is directly determined and controlled by the operator. Effective training is therefore essential.

Automatic control machines: The time which the machine spends on each of the three operations, washing, rinsing and sterilizing, is pre-set by the manufacturer. Each batch therefore receives the same effective cleansing process.

Selection of a machine will depend upon:
- the type of washing-up to be completed;
- the capabilities of the staff who will use the machine;
- the frequency with which the machine will be used;
- the rack capacity and through-put of racks per hour;
- the space available for the installation of the machine.

Catering Hygiene

Food poisoning is still not infrequent and can result from a number of causes, but it can be avoided just as easily — as shown below.

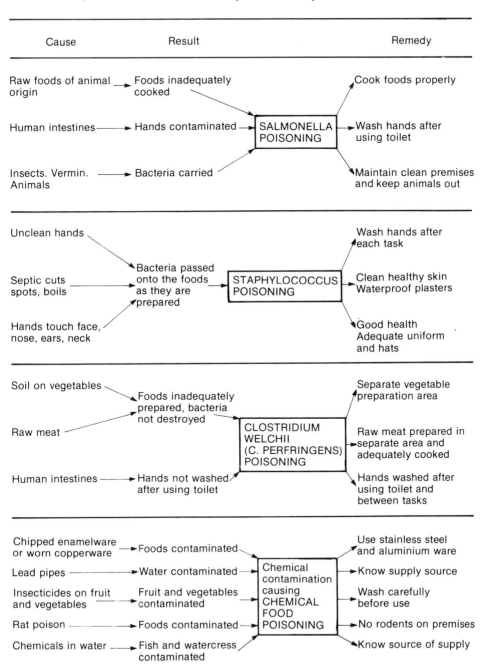

Cause	Result		Remedy
Raw foods of animal origin	Foods inadequately cooked		Cook foods properly
Human intestines	Hands contaminated	SALMONELLA POISONING	Wash hands after using toilet
Insects. Vermin. Animals	Bacteria carried		Maintain clean premises and keep animals out
Unclean hands			Wash hands after each task
Septic cuts spots, boils	Bacteria passed onto the foods as they are prepared	STAPHYLOCOCCUS POISONING	Clean healthy skin Waterproof plasters
Hands touch face, nose, ears, neck			Good health Adequate uniform and hats
Soil on vegetables	Foods inadequately prepared, bacteria not destroyed		Separate vegetable preparation area
Raw meat		CLOSTRIDIUM WELCHII (C. PERFRINGENS) POISONING	Raw meat prepared in separate area and adequately cooked
Human intestines	Hands not washed after using toilet		Hands washed after using toilet and between tasks
Chipped enamelware or worn copperware	Foods contaminated		Use stainless steel and aluminium ware
Lead pipes	Water contaminated	Chemical contamination causing CHEMICAL FOOD POISONING	Know supply source
Insecticides on fruit and vegetables	Fruit and vegetables contaminated		Wash carefully before use
Rat poison	Foods contaminated		No rodents on premises
Chemicals in water	Fish and watercress contaminated		Know source of supply

Hygiene Rules

Temperature — Foods should be either hot, at above 63°C, or cold, straight from the refrigerator.

Reheated foods — If necessary to use, they should be reheated quickly and thoroughly then consumed immediately.

Personal — Clean habits should be practised at all times.

Hands — Should be clean and well kept. No cuts or grazes.

— They should be washed frequently, especially after visiting the toilet.

Fingers — No rings, nail varnish, bitten, split, or long nails.

Health — Persons dealing with food should be of good health.

— Hair should be short and in good condition.

— Skin should be clear of all spots, boils and open wounds.

Habits — No smoking or chewing of gum is permitted in food areas as it causes the hand to be placed to the mouth and looks offensive.

Kitchen — Equipment and work surfaces should always be kept as clean as possible; cleaning should be properly organised on a rota.

Foods — All foods should be of sound quality and as fresh as possible. They should be stored safely and correctly, to avoid contamination.

Refuse — All rubbish should be cleared away and never allowed to accumulate.

Animals — No animals are permitted in food areas. Insects, flies, and rodents should be eliminated.

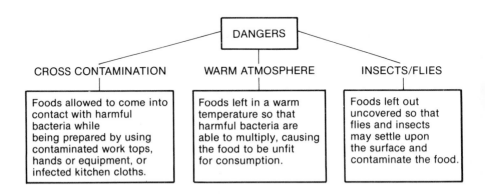

DANGERS		
CROSS CONTAMINATION	WARM ATMOSPHERE	INSECTS/FLIES
Foods allowed to come into contact with harmful bacteria while being prepared by using contaminated work tops, hands or equipment, or infected kitchen cloths.	Foods left in a warm temperature so that harmful bacteria are able to multiply, causing the food to be unfit for consumption.	Foods left out uncovered so that flies and insects may settle upon the surface and contaminate the food.

Pest Control

Type	Description	Area found	Infestation	Treatment
Rats	24cm body 20cm tail Brown/black	Sewers, grease traps, lift shafts, coal stores, dustbins	Droppings Gnawing marks Sight	Clean grease traps daily Clean bin areas daily Secure bin lids. Check exterior pointing on brickwork. Check all deliveries of coal
Mice	9cm body 8cm tail Brown/grey	Dark areas — cupboards, lofts, beneath floor boards	Droppings Damaged food and gnawing marks	Clean premises, kept well lit. Building in good repair, with stock rotation
House flies	8mm long Brown/black	Any areas where open food is evident Dustbins	Sight Noise Eggs	Eliminate any possible breeding grounds/areas. Clean bins daily. Keep lids on bins and keep them cool. Ultra-violet insect repellant lamps
Cockroach	20mm long Black/brown	Warm moist dark areas Unclean areas Sweet foods Food stores	Damaged food stocks Sight, noise and smell	Eliminate breeding areas Clean bin areas. Check structure of premises Correct food storage Rotation of stock
Silverfish	19mm long Silver/grey	Damp areas Around sinks and drains Cellulose and starchy foods	Sight Damaged foods	Check the structure of the premises and areas that are prone to dampness Ventilate sinks and all cupboard areas
Ants	3–5mm long Dark brown/red	Cracks in walls. Near food and warmth	Sight Eggs	Check the structure of the premises and the pointing of brickwork Clean premises
Wasps	2cm long Black/ yellow	Food areas Sweet items	Noise Sight Spoilt foods	Screen windows. Cover food. Ultraviolet insect repellant

Catering Legislation — A Summary

Health and Safety at Work Act 1974

Legal obligations of employers:
- to ensure the health and safety of employees;
- to provide a safe area of work and safe machines and tools to work with;
- to provide instruction and training for staff;
- to write a company safety policy document.

Legal obligations of employees:
- to take reasonable care for own health and safety;
- to take reasonable care of other persons' health and safety;
- not to mis-use any premises or equipment in the interest of health and safety.

National Insurance (Industrial Injuries) Act 1965

Relevant to all employees; it provides benefit in cases of personal injury, industrial disease, or death in the course of employment. Any claim must be made within 3 years of the injury.

Offices, Shops and Railway Premises Act 1963

This applies to any premises concerned with the sale of food and drink for immediate consumption. It relates to the cleanliness of the premises, the numbers of people in any one area, the temperature, lighting and ventilation in a work area, staff rest-rooms, first-aid facilities, protection guards on all dangerous machines, and the provision of adequate instruction for staff prior to the use of such machines, provided they are over the age of 18 years.

Food and Drugs Act 1955

This relates to the supply of food sold for human consumption, which must be in a fit condition, and properly packaged and labelled.

Food Hygiene Regulations 1970

These relate to food premises, personal hygiene, and hygienic practices.

Food premises:
- Buildings must be clean and in good repair. Hot and cold water should be available.
- Toilets must be adequate and clean, with hand washing facilities.
- First-aid and clothing lockers must be available.
- Equipment and storage areas should be in good condition.

Personal hygiene:
- Food handlers must be clean, have clean habits, and be in good health.

Hygienic practices:
- Food must be stored adequately and suitably packaged.
- No live animals are permitted in food areas.
- The Environmental Health Officer is responsible for investigating outbreaks of food poisoning.

First Aid

Principles:
- To sustain life, to prevent a casualty's condition from becoming worse, and to help recovery;
- No treatment should be given by an unqualified person — further harm may be sustained by giving unsuitable treatment;
- Nosebleeds — sit up, lean forward, and pinch the soft part of the nose.
- Burns/scalds — run under cold water to cool down the area.
- Object in eye — bathe in clean tepid water.
- Fainting — sit down with head forward and ensure air passages are not blocked.

Rules:
- Call expert help if in any doubt;
- Keep the patient calm and reassured, never leave them unattended;
- Keep the patient warm and do not move a seriously injured person;
- Never give any medication or liquid except clean water.

Legislation (The Offices, Shops, And Railway Premises First Aid Order 1964):
- There must be one first-aid box for every 150 persons employed in a premises covered by the Act, including office and administration areas of hotels, public areas of hotels, restaurants, bars, cafeterias, and public houses;
- Every box must be placed in charge of a responsible person;
- For every 150 employed persons there must be a qualified first-aid attendant, who is named on the first-aid box, to make it easy for contact in an emergency;
- First-aid boxes should be checked regularly and refilled to comply with the legislation;
- First-aid boxes should be placed in staff work areas so that they are easily accessible — kitchen, office, restaurant service area, still room, bar service area, housekeeping service rooms, staff rest-room, and front office area.

First aid boxes should contain the following basic items:
- Sterilized unmedicated dressings — finger, medium and large sizes;
- Adhesive wound dressings of assorted sizes;
- Adhesive plaster — roll 2.5cm in width;
- Triangular calico bandage;
- Sterilized cotton wool;
- Sterilized eye pad;
- Rubber/pressure bandage;
- Safety pins, scissors, eye bath, and tweezers.

It should be remembered that items will only be sterile if the pack is still sealed; as soon as it is opened it will no longer be a sterile dressing. Small individual sealed dressings are therefore normally supplied.

Food Storage

Reasons:
- It is possible to obtain basic stocks in bulk quantities.
- To obtain acceptable versatility it is necessary to have items readily available.
- Suppliers usually have set delivery days for each area.

Categories of food stored:
- Dry — cereals, pastas, flours, tea, coffee, sugars, pulses, and preserves.
- Canned — meats, fish, fruit, and vegetables.
- Dairy — eggs, fats, cheese, and bacon.
- Frozen — meats, fish, poultry, vegetables, fruit, ice cream, and cream.
- Fresh — fruit, vegetables, milk, and cream.

Types of supplier:
- Wholesaler for dry goods and frozen goods.
- Cash-and-carry warehouse for dry and frozen goods.
- Market for specialist or seasonal items.
- Dairy for milk, cream, and eggs.

Methods of payment:
- Contract price that is negotiated for a set figure over a number of months.
- Monthly account that is presented for payment at the end of each month.
- Cash paid for the goods at a cash-and-carry warehouse.

Store room:
- It must be dry, cool, well ventilated, and light.
- It must have adequate shelving and space for foods.
- The refrigeration must be efficient.
- An honest, methodical storekeeper must be employed.

Control of stock:
- To reduce risk of pilferage.
- To ensure that the stock is in good condition when required.
- To reduce food wastage, and to encourage the economical use of foods.
- To ensure accurate food costings.

Methods of Stock Control

Bin Cards	Computerised	Stock sheets
One card per item, which names the supplier, restocking level, quantity to order, unit cost, and total quantity of stock in-hand. The value of stock may be calculated at any time.	Stock held, issued, and received is monitored and the figures are instantly available. Recall figures to compare with purchases and trading in any previous period. But expensive to install.	Record all items received and issued. Total cash value and stock level is on a weekly basis, giving weekly trading figures. But time consuming to total up.

Unit 8 Assessment Activities

1. (a) Analyse the work flow patterns in the kitchen where you work.
   (b) Identify any areas that could be the cause of an accident and recommend ways of eliminating these hazards.

2. Write a set of catering hygiene rules and use these to design a poster for a staff room.

3. Draw a picture of a chef, labelling all the parts that could either cause an accident or a hygiene hazard if he was not correctly dressed.

4. (a) Describe what is meant by cross contamination in a kitchen.
   (b) State how this can occur and how it can be prevented.

5. (a) Describe how all types of food should be stored in a catering unit.
   (b) State why correct food storage is an important part of a storekeeper's work.

Unit 9:

Food Service

Types of establishments
Marketing and menu planning
Hospital food service systems
Food service equipment
Tableware
Traditional ancillary departments
Food service staff
Guests with special needs
The restaurant brigade
Traditional forms of service
Cafeteria service
Portion control
Assessment activities

Types of Establishments

Type of unit	Contribution	Facilities	Staff and duties
Take-Away Fish and chips Pizzas Pancakes Burgers Fried chicken Ethnic — Indian, Chinese	Reasonably priced, quick snack food available all day Standard quality and menu	May have seating facilities for some people Menu displayed outside and inside in a large print Foods cooked as ordered	• Supervisor — responsible for daily operation of unit • Food production staff — cook partially prepared foods using standard methods • General assistants — may take orders, serve foods, clear tables, wash up
Transport Café Traditional type snacks and substantial meals	Reasonably priced meals For lorry drivers and travellers	Large lorry/van parking area. Toilets Telephone. Reasonable comfort level Cafeteria service	• Cook/manager — responsible for unit, costs, foods, staffing and cooking • General assistants — serve foods, clear away, wash up
Motorway Eating Quick snacks Meals Grills Restaurants	Reasonably priced foods No alcohol provided Open 24 hours per day, 7 days per week	Cafeteria-style units Waitress-service restaurants. Quick snack food areas Toilets, telephones and shop. Large parks for cars, coaches, lorries Garage petrol sales	• Manager — complete control • Assistant manager — assist manager • Chef/cook — prepare foods • General assistants — help in kitchens to prepare and serve foods and snacks • Table clearers — clear and clean tables, wash up • Waitresses — wait on tables
Restaurants in Retail Stores Meals Snacks Coffee shops	Facilities for shoppers and families to eat Encourages business in the store	Waitress or self- service type units Morning coffee, luncheons, teas, snacks. Toilets and telephones	• Manager — complete control • Cook — prepares foods • Assistants — help in all sections, preparing, serving, clearing, washing up • Waitresses — serve foods

Types of Establishments (Continued)

Type of unit	Contribution	Facilities	Staff and duties
Restaurants — Independents or in Hotels			
General foods Speciality dishes Ethnic foods Traditional foods	Selection of foods for the general public and business people May be special functions or dinners	À la carte and table d'hôte style menu choice in waitress service restaurants May be licensed to sell alcohol	• Manager — complete responsibility for unit • Chef — preparation of all foods, standards of unit • Assistants — help in all areas of food preparation • Waiters — service of all foods and drinks
Industrial Canteens			
Meals and snacks Beverages Usually subsidised by the employer	Meals, snacks and all types of beverages for employees while at work Inexpensive prices	Cafeteria-style of service, with a small dining room for the senior staff and for business luncheons Beverages from trolley or vending machines Confectionery sales	• Manager — responsible for catering unit and staff • Chef/cook — preparation of meals in all areas • Assistants — help in all food preparation areas Service of beverages from trolleys. Washing up • Waitresses — service of meals in dining room areas
Railways — Trains			
Main meals Snack food Limited to some routes and times of day	Snacks and beverages for all travellers Limited to some trains Some alcohol	Limited seating and waiter service for main meals, may be restricted to type of ticket traveller has purchased. Beverages and some confectionery sales	• Chief Steward — responsible for food and cash on the train, and the staff • Chef — preparation of meals • Stewards — service of meals and snacks in the buffet car and along the train. Clearing up in buffet car

Types of Establishments (Continued)

Type of unit	Contribution	Facilities	Staff and duties
Railway Stations and Airports			
Main meals and snacks Take-away foods Beverages Limited alcohol licence	Snacks and meals for all travellers while waiting for departure Staff employed at stations and airports	Cafeteria and full waiter service may be available. Breakfasts, teas, lunches, coffees, confectionery, sandwiches, beverages	• Manager — control of unit • Cook — preparation of foods • Assistants — help in all areas with food preparation service and clearing away • Waiters — service of foods in restaurants
Airlines			
Main meals, snacks and beverages Alcohol Crew meals	All meals and snacks for the passengers and the crew	Trayed meals — limited choice Beverages and limited choice of snacks and drinks available. Ethnic foods by prior request only	• Chief Steward — responsible for the catering while in flight. Crew served different foods from passengers • Stewards — service of all food and drink to passengers
Ocean Liners			
Restaurants Coffee shops Snack bars Licensed bars Crew cafeterias	All meals and snacks for the passengers and the crew while at sea	Choice of standard type of meals in various types of restaurants and bars. May be restricted by type of ticket the traveller has purchased	• Food and beverage manager and a full brigade of staff for the kitchen and the restaurant, to staff the different facilities on board the liner

Marketing and Menu Planning

Marketing

There are many considerations that need thought before planning or launching a new catering establishment, or simply updating an existing unit. The trends for the future indicate a faster service, less formality, less staff employed, and tight target costs. For these reasons the following aspects need consideration:
• The image and atmosphere of the establishment;
• The type of customer that is likely to be attracted to the establishment and their likely expectations;

166

- The size and situation of the nearest car park and its likely capacity;
- Alcoholic licence, if this is to be a facility offered to the customer;
- Likely opening times and staff availability at these times;
- Competition from neighbouring outlets;
- Local market days and early closing day;
- Likely weather — the geographical situation within the country;
- Likely peak times and months of the year for maximum customers;
- Ethnic customs and feast days.

Menu planning

To achieve customer satisfaction menus should be planned with the following considerations:

Costs
- Costs must be kept within specified limits.
- Meat and fish are the most expensive forms of protein; if the costs are to be kept low, other forms of protein should be used in the menus.

Staff Capability
- The staff must be able to cook and prepare the menu.
- The menu content should extend the staff skills and thereby ensure job satisfaction for the staff.

Time available
- There must be enough time available for adequate preparation and cooking of the foods.
- There must be sufficient time to serve the foods to their best advantage.
- If foods have to be kept hot before they are to be served, there must be suitable facilities so as not to spoil the finished product.

Equipment
- The equipment should be utilized to its full potential.
- There should be a wide range of cooking methods to ensure that all equipment is fully used.

Nutrition
- In some catering outlets the nutritional value of the meal is a prime consideration, such as in hospitals, schools, etc.
- The foods selected must provide the daily nutritional requirements in welfare establishments.
- There should always be a balance between protein foods, foods that contain protective elements, and those with a high carbohydrate content.
- Fibre is an essential part of any meal and customers are now more aware of the fibre content of their foods.

- Animal fat is considered by some people to be harmful if eaten in excessive quantities; some consideration as to the fat content of the meal is therefore necessary.

Variety
- Each menu should provide customer satisfaction by giving a variety of textures, shapes and sizes.
- The foods should provide a good range of colour to create an attractive appearance on the plate.

Season
- Seasonal foods should be used to increase interest and variety of taste into the menu.
- When using fresh foods, care should be taken that the nutrients are not destroyed by poor handling or over-cooking.

Customers
- The type of customer should be considered; religious and ethnic tastes should be appreciated and catered for.

Hospital Food Service Sytems

The ganymede system

This is used for the service of hospital patients' meals:

Day 1	Day 2	Day 3
Patients select their choice of meals for Day 2.	Orders co-ordinated. Chef prepares the meals ordered.	Food taken from cook/freeze unit or storage areas. Patients select meals for following day.

It works in the following way:

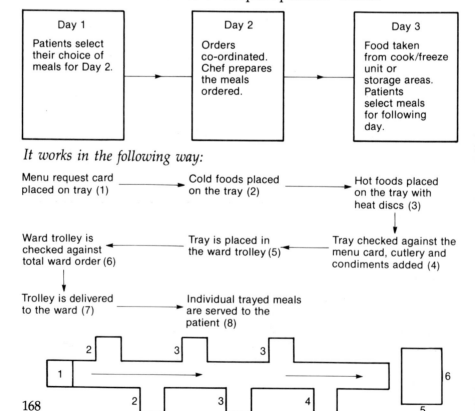

Menu request card placed on tray (1) → Cold foods placed on the tray (2) → Hot foods placed on the tray with heat discs (3)

Ward trolley is checked against total ward order (6) ← Tray is placed in the ward trolley (5) ← Tray checked against the menu card, cutlery and condiments added (4)

Trolley is delivered to the ward (7) → Individual trayed meals are served to the patient (8)

- The conveyor belt is a permanent fixture in the food service area of the catering complex.
- There are various sizes and designs of mobile service units that are filled and then wheeled into position along the length of the conveyor belt as they are ready.
- The mobile units are designed to take complete racks of small dishes and bowls, stacks of plates, lids and trays, and have a spring self-levelling mechanism, so that the stack rises as the top few items are removed and used.
- Foods are kept hot by the use of small heat-retaining discs that are placed under each plate of food on the tray. This will keep the patient's food hot while it is being taken to the ward and while it is actually being eaten; so a complete three-course hot meal can be placed on a tray and kept hot.
- Each plate or bowl of food is topped with an appropriate-sized stainless steel lid.
- Cutlery and sachets of condiments are then added to the tray, together with the menu card that the patient completed when he requested his meal choice.

Advantages	Disadvantages
<ul><li>The patient has individually trayed meals served to him for each meal.</li><li>The patient has a choice of foods for each meal.</li><li>It is quick to serve on the ward and looks attractive.</li><li>Accurate food costing, as the menu choice is known the day before it is required.</li><li>Foods are kept hot for a minimum length of time.</li></ul>	<ul><li>When the patient is first admitted he has to accept the meal that has already been selected by the ward staff.</li><li>Standard portions served in the kitchen means that there are no second helpings available in the wards.</li><li>The patient cannot change his mind once the meal has been selected.</li><li>The complete meal is placed before the patient, which may tend to put him off his food if he sees too much on the tray.</li></ul>

How it works

Patients
- The aim is to increase the patient's recovery rate by providing well prepared, nutritious, well-balanced, attractive meals at regular intervals to all patients staying in the hospital.
- Central preparation from one main kitchen area may either use the cook/chill/freeze process, or the more traditional methods of preparation.

- The ganymede system of traying the individual patient's meals is frequently used to ensure that the food reaches the patients in the best possible condition.
- Special diets are prepared for any patients that need this facility, in the diet kitchen with trained diet cooks, under the direction of the hospital dietician.
- The meals are delivered to the wards in trolleys and then served to the patients in the wards by the ward staff, either in the day-room or to patients in their beds. The pre-selection of meals will increase the patient's enjoyment of and satisfaction with the food.
- Beverages are normally prepared by the ward staff in their ward kitchen.

Staff
- There are catering facilities of all types available during the day and evening, with reduced facilities available at night-time.
- Consultants, doctors, and other senior staff grades have a quiet waitress-service dining room.
- Most other staff use either cafeteria-style service or take advantage of the snacks that are available near their lounge areas.
- Vending and microwave units are increasingly used at night-times for staff meals and hot snacks.

Food Service Equipment

When selecting equipment the following points must be considered:

Large items
- Type of service and therefore the space required for side-tables, trolleys, etc.
- Existing features and furnishings, colours, textures, image of premises.
- Versatility of use to allow for different types of service and functions.
- Tables — linked, shape, size, height, seating number, top surface.
- Chairs — height to table, stackable, comfortable, easily cleaned.
- Cleaning — new techniques, skills or equipment needed to clean adequately.
- Replaceable, continuing designs, easily re-ordered.
- Complementary colours and materials in daylight and artificial light.
- Fixed or free-standing furniture, legs, casters.
- Strong and durable; check design of the legs' supports and casters.

Small items

Flatware	Cutlery	Glassware
Size and shape	Method of washing	Storage area, shelf height
Multi-purpose design	Storage facilities	Washing method, rack size
Style of service	Number of covers	Range of drinks served
Type of menu	Turn round time	Versatility of uses
Number of covers	Type of service	Percentage of each drink sold
Turn round time	Type of menu	Replacement designs
Size of storage area	Versatility of use	Delivery numbers/times/costs
Size of machine racks	Limited grooves/pattern	Easily handled/correct service
Design/style of	Silver/stainless steel	Limited pattern/easy cleaning
restaurant	Handles of bone/steel	Design and style of premises
Embossed house logo	House logo embossed	Strong/toughened glass

Restaurant linen

Before deciding whether to use traditional linen or disposable linen, the following points should be considered.

— *Traditional*
- Style of restaurant.
- Made from: linen/cotton/polyester/terylene.
- Laundry facilities.
- Colour scheme.
- Availability of replacements.
- Dual purpose sizes.
- Type of service.
- Number of covers.

— *Disposable*
- Cost — contract with price guaranteed.
- Delivery quantities and times.
- Availability of continuous supplies.
- Continuity of colour and style.
- Quality and ply thickness.
- House logo printed, or name and address.
- Refuse disposal methods, incinerator/waste compactor.
- Customer acceptance.

Tableware

Materials used

Earthenware — Glazed earthenware is used in the hotel trade. Fireproof earthenware, for oven to table ware, is used for bar snack trade and for microwave items.

Stoneware — It is heavy and thick and stands a considerable amount of hard wear. Vitreous stoneware, or ironware, is stronger and is commonly used for everyday catering tableware.

China/porcelain — A delicate material that is liable to chip and break. It is attractive but not strong enough for the catering trade.

Artificial porcelain — It is stronger than true porcelain and makes attractive tableware.

Stainless steel — It is an alloy containing 13 per cent chromium. Staybrite contains nickel and chromium. It is widely used for cutlery and tableware and for dishes. It does not stain unless misused or over-heated.

Silver — Usually this metal is silver plated and used for ornate cutlery and tableware. It is more expensive than stainless steel and will scratch more easily. It will become tarnished quickly and therefore requires more cleaning and maintenance than stainless steel.

Types of Cutlery

Item	Uses
Soup spoon	Soup when served in a soup plate. Irish stew.
Fish knives/forks	Fish courses. Fish as a main course. Hors d'oeuvres.
Large knives/forks	Entrée and main courses.
Large forks	Used on their own for omelets, macaroni, gnocchi.
Fork and dessert spoon	Spaghetti dishes.
Dessert spoon/fork	All sweets served on plates. Oeufs sur le plat.
Dessert spoon	On its own for soup served in cups, breakfast cereals, porridge.
Small knives/forks	Ornate handles, short blades, for dessert fruit course.
Small knives	Used with 15cm plate for bread rolls, toast, cheese/biscuits.
Small knives/forks	Used with savoury course items with a 20cm plate.
Tea spoons	Tea. Morning coffee. Fruit cocktails, ice cream coupes. Oeufs en cocotte.
Coffee spoons	Used with demi-tasse cups of coffee.
Small tea knives	Small-sized for afternoon tea service.
Sundae spoons	Oval bowl, small-sized, used with ice cream desserts.
Table spoons	Service of foods onto the plates — often used with a large fork.
Pastry fork	Used for pastries when served with mid-morning coffee.

Types of Tableware

Type	Capacity/shape	Uses
Side plate	15cm round	Bread items. Cheese. Small savouries. Afternoon teas. Pastries.
Entrée plate	20cm round	Hors d'oeuvres. Single fish dishes. Desserts. Fruits.
Dinner plate	25cm round	Main meals
Grill plate	30cm oval	Grill specialities. Whole fish.
Soup plate	23cm round, shallow	Soup. Irish stew.
Soup bowl	13cm round, deep	Soup. Breakfast cereals.
Dessert plate	13cm round, deep	Desserts, hot puddings.
Soup cup/saucer	Circular, 2 handles, saucer	Consommé
Tea cup/saucer	5 to a litre	Tea. Morning coffee. Evening drinks.
Demi-tasse cup	10 to a litre	Coffee after luncheon or dinner.

General care

- Always store tableware in areas with impervious surfaces.
- Store in areas that are free from dust contamination.
- Store in situations that are free from condensation and grease.
- Eliminate all unnecessary handling and contamination by hands.
- Shelves should be labelled to encourage tidy storage of items.
- All storage rooms and cupboards should be checked regularly.
- Storage areas should be locked after service times as the stock value is high and small items may go missing.
- Tableware and cutlery should never be used in the kitchen preparation areas as it will become dented, scratched, and damaged.
- Ashtrays and flower vases should be separately washed and stored on trays to eliminate the risk of contaminating the tableware.
- Teapots and coffee jugs need regular de-scaling inside to remove the tannin stains and water scale.
- Cruets need to be emptied regularly and cleaned then dried and refilled.
- Oil and vinegar bottles will become sticky if not washed regularly.
- Sugar sifters will absorb moisture if not kept absolutely dry.
- Cutlery should be stored in divided trays, away from any dust or grease.
- Glassware should be stored inverted in racks or on shelves.
- Service dishes should be stored in stacks of tens, with their lids next to each pile. Flat dishes should be piled according to size.

Traditional Ancillary Departments

These are found in larger hotels and restaurants to eliminate non-cooking tasks from being carried out in the kitchen, as these can cause unnecessary congestion at peak times of the day and disruption to the food production staff.

The stillroom

This is found in large establishments, next to the restaurant and near to the lounge areas. In small establishments an area of either the service room or the kitchen may be equipped to provide these items away from the main food preparation areas.

The purpose and function of the stillroom is as follows:

Restaurant
- Breakfast-time preparation of tea, coffee, and beverages. The provision of toast, breakfast cereals, butter and preserves.
- Luncheon time preparation of coffee, the provision of butter, brown bread and butter, and melba toast.
- Dinner/evening service, the provision of coffee, butter pats, toast, and after dinner mints.

Lounge
- Mid-morning provision of coffees and pastries.
- Afternoon preparation of tea, sandwiches, scones and cakes.
- Evening provision of hot drinks, tea, coffee, and milk-based beverages.

The equipment likely to be found in a stillroom includes the following:
(a) Boiling water point
(b) Steam injection unit for milk
(c) Coffee-making equipment
(d) Toast-making equipment
(e) Refrigerator
(f) Cash and billing equipment
(g) Sandwich-making equipment
(h) Washing-up machine or area
(i) Refuse disposal facilities
(j) Storage area for food commodities
(k) Cutlery, crockery, trays, napkins and doilies.

The service area

This is a space found between the kitchen and the restaurant to keep the food production free from the washing up of tableware, collection of linen, and the disposal of restaurant refuse.

The Advantages of a Still room	The Advantages of a Service Area
• Staff are able to keep a stock of items ready for the food service staff to collect.	• Food service staff can obtain replacement linen, cutlery, crockery and glassware as and when they are needed.
• Condiments, such as salt, are not subjected to the steam and heat of the kitchens.	• All used tableware from the restaurant can be deposited in the service room before the staff enter the kitchen to collect their next order. Clean items can be collected at the same time.
• Morning coffee and afternoon tea trade can be expanded without the use of the main kitchen.	
• Cash and stock can be controlled separately to give precise costings.	

Food Service Staff

Body language is the main method of non-verbal communication used in restaurants, both between the waiting staff and the guests and the waiting staff themselves. It is necessary to be aware of these actions and to understand the effect that these actions may have upon other people, in particular the customers. There are both positive and negative actions.

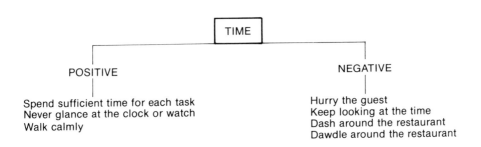

TIME

POSITIVE

Spend sufficient time for each task
Never glance at the clock or watch
Walk calmly

NEGATIVE

Hurry the guest
Keep looking at the time
Dash around the restaurant
Dawdle around the restaurant

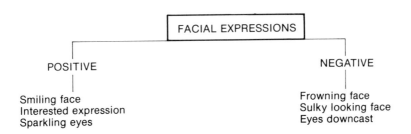

FACIAL EXPRESSIONS

POSITIVE

Smiling face
Interested expression
Sparkling eyes

NEGATIVE

Frowning face
Sulky looking face
Eyes downcast

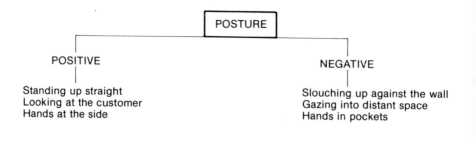

POSTURE

POSITIVE

Standing up straight
Looking at the customer
Hands at the side

NEGATIVE

Slouching up against the wall
Gazing into distant space
Hands in pockets

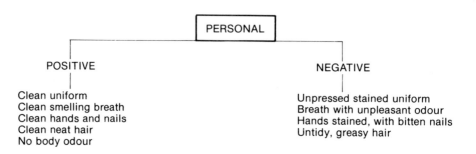

PERSONAL

POSITIVE

Clean uniform
Clean smelling breath
Clean hands and nails
Clean neat hair
No body odour

NEGATIVE

Unpressed stained uniform
Breath with unpleasant odour
Hands stained, with bitten nails
Untidy, greasy hair

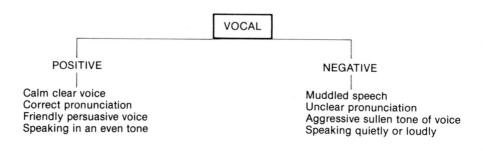

VOCAL

POSITIVE

Calm clear voice
Correct pronunciation
Friendly persuasive voice
Speaking in an even tone

NEGATIVE

Muddled speech
Unclear pronunciation
Aggressive sullen tone of voice
Speaking quietly or loudly

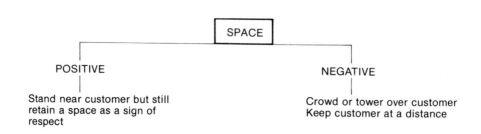

SPACE

POSITIVE

Stand near customer but still
retain a space as a sign of
respect

NEGATIVE

Crowd or tower over customer
Keep customer at a distance

176

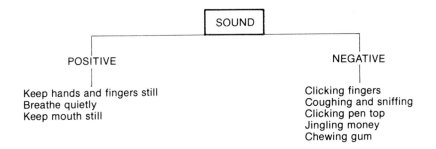

SOUND

POSITIVE

Keep hands and fingers still
Breathe quietly
Keep mouth still

NEGATIVE

Clicking fingers
Coughing and sniffing
Clicking pen top
Jingling money
Chewing gum

The restaurant team

All work in a restaurant is a type of team work, with each member of staff dependent on others for the successful completion of his tasks. Staff can have a helpful positive method and approach or a negative unhelpful attitude.

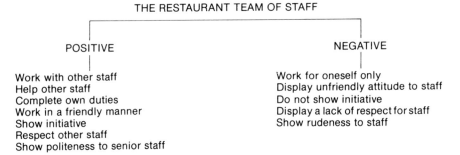

THE RESTAURANT TEAM OF STAFF

POSITIVE

Work with other staff
Help other staff
Complete own duties
Work in a friendly manner
Show initiative
Respect other staff
Show politeness to senior staff

NEGATIVE

Work for oneself only
Display unfriendly attitude to staff
Do not show initiative
Display a lack of respect for staff
Show rudeness to staff

All food service personnel need to have the type of qualities that will enable them to work as part of a team, and to serve the guests in a manner that will ensure that they enjoy their meal to its full potential. They must:

- Believe in the product that they are selling and serving.
- Be persuasive but never aggressive towards the guest.
- Be well groomed and create an efficient image.
- Be warm towards other people and be genuinely pleased to see them.
- Like people and like serving and selling to them.
- Give a genuine and not a false impression.
- Remember and recognise regular customers.
- Retain knowledge of the menu and the other services offered.
- Demonstrate an awareness of the guests' needs.

Guests with Special Needs

Catering for guests with special needs calls for a caring attitude from the food service staff and foresight in the planning stages of the establishment. The food service staff should always maintain as normal a service as possible but with some definite considerations, particularly when the guest first comes into the restaurant.

Elderly guests
- There must be easy access to their table and the cloakrooms.
- An upright chair or one with arms may be required.
- Place this type of guest in the restaurant where there is a good view of everything, they will not like a dark alcoved area.

Blind guests
- There must be easy access to their table.
- Place them in the restaurant where no one sound or smell is dominant.
- Place them at a table where they will not be bumped or knocked by other persons passing their table.
- Facilities must be provided for their guide dog and cane; the dog will appreciate a drink of water.
- The food service staff should always offer to read the menu to the guest.

Deaf guests
- Place the guest where they can see as much as possible.
- Place the guest where there are even sound levels, away from loud speakers, music outlets or telephones.
- Staff should always listen carefully to the guest's voice, as it may not be very clear.

Wheelchair guests
- Easy access into the restaurant is essential.
- Adequate turning space for the wheelchair is necessary.
- Place the guest at a table where they may see as much of the restaurant as possible.
- They should never be placed away in a corner or just by the exit area.

Catering for the young

In areas where families frequent the restaurant there may be a special children's menu to encourage this family custom. It ensures that the children are served with foods that they can appreciate. With young children in a formal restaurant the food service staff need to encourage the child's quiet undisruptive behaviour by:
- giving the child a high chair or a cushion to sit upon;
- placing the child where it can see plenty going on;
- placing the family where potential noise will cause least disturbance.

The Restaurant Brigade

Waiter service is used in many different types of establishment and there are many styles of service used in restaurants. Each establishment uses a variation on one or more of the four basic types of service. These are known as: table d'hôte, à la carte, guéridon, and family service. Not all restaurants have the full traditional brigade or team of waiting staff, as listed below; many have a less well defined job description to enable the restaurant to be run with a versatile skilled team of food service personnel.

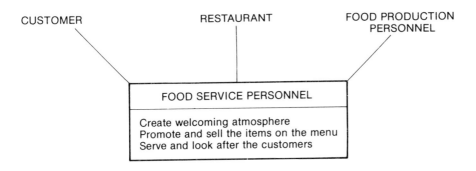

Restaurant Manager — Responsible for the organization and supervision of all the work in the restaurant, and for his team of staff.
Head Waiter — Will greet the customers and show them to their table. He supervises the food service staff.
Station Head Waiter — Responsible for an area of the restaurant, he will receive the customers and take their menu orders.
Wine Waiter — Will advise upon and take orders for all alcoholic drinks, and also serve all wines and other beverages.
Station Waiter — Responsible for the service of the foods ordered in an area of the restaurant.
Junior Waiter — Will generally assist the station waiter in the service of foods to the guests in that section.
Assistant Waiter — A very junior position, he will assist in the clearing, fetching, and carrying for the other waiters.

Traditional Forms of Service

Table d'hôte

In this form of menu or service the full range of cutlery is laid and then removed should the guest not require that particular course. The menu is a fixed price, offering some choice within each course. This type of menu gives the customer a choice of dishes, whilst eliminating the wastage that could occur when an extensive menu choice is used. It may also reduce the size of the kitchen brigade.

À la carte

In this form of menu the minimum of crockery and cutlery is laid upon the table; any additional items are laid as the choice of the guests dictates. The choice is extensive and usually priced by each item. The meal is often more expensive and tends to be prepared to order, so the service time is lengthened. These factors mean that the use of microwave ovens, convection ovens and high pressure steamers in the kitchen is essential to produce a good quality meal that is individually prepared when it is ordered.

Guéridon service

A form of personalised service often used with an à la carte or a table d'hôte menu. The food is carved or finished at a table or trolley placed adjacent to the guest's table. A spirit lamp is used to finish cooking portions of poultry, meat or fish. Some dishes are completed in this way with a flambé technique or sauce: vegetables may be tossed in butter or sauce and then served to accompany the meal; sweet dishes and fruits may be finished in a similar manner, one of the most popular being the preparation and service of Crêpes Suzette. This form of service requires a skilled team of staff who can complete the cooking of the foods as the menu and form of service requires, can present and serve the foods in an efficient and pleasing manner to the guest, and possess the air of quiet confidence and salesmanship.

Plated/family service

A less formal form of service used with table d'hôte menus. Here the main meal is presented to the customer on a 25cm diameter plate; the accompanying vegetables may either be placed on the plate in the kitchen, or placed in vegetable dishes on the table — allowing the guest to help himself. Full plated service promotes fast efficient service and ensures good portion control. The guest may, however, prefer to help himself to vegetables and accompaniments, so that he is not faced with a full plate of food at any one time. Plated service is used in cafeteria service, where the customer may help himself or be served by staff at the hot plate.

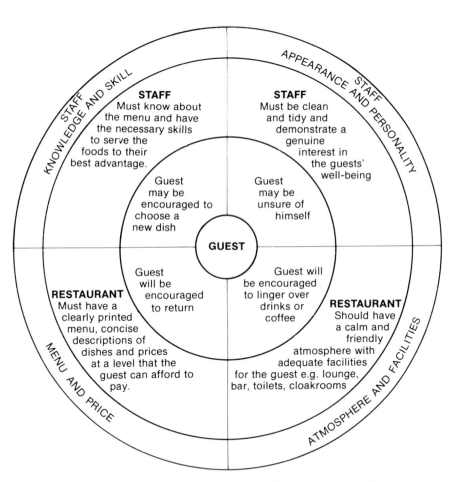

The influence of the restaurant and staff upon the guest

Cafeteria Service

Self-service is a quick form of service used in cafeterias, where the customers select their food from the displayed area and pay for it before taking their trays to a vacant table, in the adjacent dining area. With this type of service there are differing tasks and roles for the food service personnel; their duties are primarily concerned with the actual serving of the foods upon request from the customers and selling the food directly to the customers, who often need encouragement to purchase items from the menu. It must be emphasised that there has to be an efficient system for replenishing the supplies of foods on the menu from the kitchen.

This type of service is found in numerous types of establishments, including schools, colleges, halls of residences, staff cafeterias in industry, hospitals and hotels. For success it is essential that the speed of service is quick and efficient. Delays may be caused for various reasons, the most common causes being:

- Cashier unable to take money and give change fast enough;
- Customer unable to make a choice of foods to purchase;
- Trays not available for customers to use for their foods;
- Foods not available because service staff have not restocked in time;
- Service staff too slow in serving the customers.

Layout

There are numerous types of cafeteria layouts. A combined hot and cold plan would normally be arranged in this basic order:

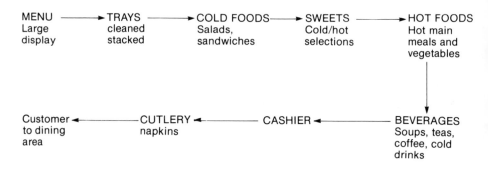

It is essential that prompt and efficient clearing is maintained in the dining area at all times. Tables that are cluttered with used crockery indicate a lack of supervision, training and hygienic practice. This will discourage customers and cause a slack attitude from the staff.

The seating capacity must be estimated to enable the throughput number of customers sitting down at any one time. This is estimated by taking the average eating time and then taking the number of meals served and finally the total service time.

To estimate cafeteria seating requirements:
Service time — 2 hours
Numbers served — 720   Average seating time — 20 minutes
Therefore the tables are used 6 times in the 2 hours.
Numbers seated at any one time, 720 divided by 6 = 120
Minimum seating needed = 120 seats
Suggested overflow = 30 seats
Total seating required = 150.

Cafeteria preparation

Preparation starts at the end of the previous day's work:
- Cashier will empty till, pay in cash, record takings, and deposit float in safe.
- General assistants will — clear food items, returning them to the kitchen.
  — clear beverages from hot and cold units.
  — clean all service areas, display cabinets, and cold shelves.
  — clean the service area, including the floor areas.
Before service starts in the morning the following tasks must be completed:
- Switch on hot plates, check contents and crockery numbers.
- Complete menu boards, check prices.
- Rinse through beverage units, refill and switch on power.
- Clean and check customer seating area.
- Place cutlery, trays, napkins, and water glasses in their places.
- Condiments and sundries prepared and placed in their positions.
- Cold foods placed in display area, and reserves in cold cabinets.
- Beverages and cups prepared.
- Hot foods placed in hot plate and bain-marie, and service utensils collected.
- Cashier prepare till, check menu, prices, and float.
- Staff in correct positions ready for service.

Cafeteria clearing methods

There are two main methods commonly used in self-service dining areas: with the use of a catering assistant and a trolley, or with the customers self-clearing their trays to a hatchway or conveyor belt. The self-clearing method is often used in welfare units, such as industrial canteens and staff cafeterias. The cafeterias that are open to the general public are normally cleared by a catering assistant and a trolley.

Trolley and catering assistant	Customer self-clearing
Trolley pushed between tables and used crockery items and trays are cleared. With a disposable cloth and hand-held spray filled with a germicidal detergent solution, the assistant will clean the tables for the next customer, without passing bacteria from one area to another. An adequate number of trolleys is essential so that one full trolley may be unloaded as a clear one is taken out by the assistant. It is necessary to wash the trolleys after each use to prevent bacterial growth.	Customers are asked to clear their own used crockery and trays when they have finished their meal. The clearing area must be placed near the exit door and positioned to prevent any cross flow of traffic between new customers and those that are leaving. Staff are required to keep this clearing area free from piles of dirty crockery and scraps of uneaten food, in order to prevent bacterial growth. The tables need to be cleaned for new customers.

The cafeteria menu

To ensure an efficient successful cafeteria service there must be adequately trained staff and suitable menus and prices for potential customers. The catering manager must consider the following aspects before deciding on a cafeteria menu:

General points:
- Preparation — the time available, the staff capabilities, the staff skills and the equipment available.
- Cooking — the ability to keep hot/cold at top quality or cook/chill and reheat upon demand in a microwave convection oven or high pressure steamer.
- Display — to create customer appeal.
  Customer recognition of dishes and acceptability of dishes. Variety of colour, texture, taste, and shape of foods.
- Menu — costs must be acceptable to the customers.
  Selection must offer a good variety of dishes to make acceptable combinations for meals.

Standard menu:
- This will give standard cost levels, preparation times, procedures and equipment requirements.

- It will allow for minimum items in stock and limited staff skills.
- The customer will become familiar with the menu and thereby ensure acceptance.

Skeleton menu:
- This will have the advantages of the standard menu with a variety of one or two items in each menu module.
- It will increase customer satisfaction and staff interest in their situation by providing variety.

Menu display

- It is the main method of attracting customers into the cafeteria area.
- It should be displayed in an attractive, clearly priced manner.
- Pictures or photographs help to sell the products.
- Parts of the menu that apply to a section of the service area are often displayed on the back wall to help with customer selection.

Portion Control

The use of acceptable portion control methods in any catering operation is an essential part of planning and cost control. It is also a useful marketing asset as the customer will not appreciate the idea of each portion being of a different size and weight yet all retail prices being the same.

Advantages of good portion control	Consequences of poor portion control
• Profit control • Accurate cost control • Customer satisfaction • Staff able to work to a standard • Low/minimum wastage level • Accurate purchasing forecasts • Minimum stock held in reserve	• Little chance of profit control • No control over food costs • Poor customer/management relations • Low standards of staff achievement • High/unpredictable wastage level • Erratic purchasing quantities • High food levels held in stock

Ensuring portion control rules

- Adequate staff training in company methods/sizes of portions.
- Good effective staff control by supervisory staff.
- Staff awareness of the reasons for portion control.
- Adequate service dishes and implements to enable the correct sizes to be used at all times.
- Display diagrams/posters of portion sizes for staff to refer to while preparing dishes in the kitchen.

Methods

- Cuts of meats are controlled by the head chef and the waiting staff will be made aware of the correct portion size, such as 2 cutlets or 3 slices per portion.
- Whole items, such as fillets of fish, are purchased by size by the head chef and therefore portions are controlled.
- Vegetables are portioned by the use of measured capacity scoops, nets, and spoons. Staff are made aware of the appropriate implement for each type of vegetable.
- Soups and sauces are portioned by the use of appropriate-sized ladles, or in some establishments the soup bowl capacity will dictate the portion size.
- Salads are portioned by the plate size, which will ensure that the finished size is correct. The mix contents will be controlled in the larder by the larder chef. Each salad should contain the same number of items.
- Pies, puddings, and items that may be cooked in varying sized containers are controlled by standard-sized dishes being used — either to create a set number of portions per dish or by using individual-sized dishes, creating one pie per person.
- Made-up items, such as bread rolls, scones, pizzas, pasties, and croquettes, are weighed prior to final shaping to ensure uniform sizes.

Unit 9 Assessment Activities

1. (a) Compile a questionnaire to find out which fast food catering outlet is most frequently used by your colleagues.
   (b) Discuss the findings of this survey in relation to the marketing and image created by the catering outlet.

2. (a) Describe the relationship between marketing and menu planning for a cafeteria service restaurant.
   (b) Draw a plan of a cafeteria service unit, indicating where the different parts of the menu are to be served from.

3. (a) Draw a diagram to show the ways that tables may be laid in different types of restaurants.
   (b) List the points that will need to be considered before selecting the most suitable way to lay up the restaurant.

4. (a) Draw a plan of a food service department to include the food preparation area, the ancillary departments, and the restaurant.
   (b) Indicate the work flow paths for the different sections of staff.

5. Design a chart to illustrate the most helpful and positive manners that food service personnel should possess and display when serving food.

Unit 10:

Food and Beverage Control

Methods of billing
Computerised control systems
Restaurant and lounge control
Service of alcoholic beverages
Wine storage and uses
Fortified wines
Beers
Spirits
Assessment activities

Methods of Billing

Adequate control of cash taken is essential as it will enable the management to:
- Forecast future trade trends.
- Ensure correct billing to customers.
- Facilitate correct costings and therefore correct charges.
- Reduce the amount of wastage by not over-producing.
- Reduce or eliminate pilferage by keeping a tight check at all times.

Fast food billing

Here the menu is limited to a standard selection.

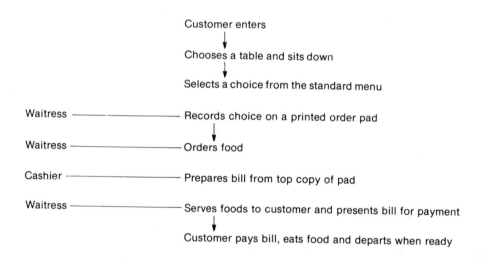

With this system the customer will have to wait while the foods that he has ordered are prepared and served to him. He will not wish to wait long and the preparation is normally a standard procedure to ensure that it may be kept to an acceptable minimum time. When the customer has eaten his foods he can leave as he has already paid the bill; this system eliminates the chance of any customer leaving the premises without paying for his meal.

Triplicate system

There are three copies of the customer's order on the waiter's pad, giving the date, table number and number of guests, as well as the foods that they have ordered.

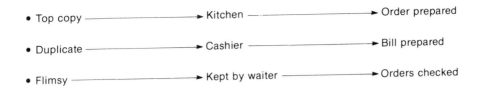

This standard system is used in many restaurants. Control is exercised by checking the top copies, the duplicates and the bill.

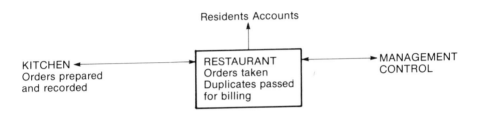

There are many types of cash registers and billing machines available for use in every type and size of outlet. Each establishment will select the cash control system that will suit their requirements.

Billing machines are in use in many restaurants; these have the following advantages:

Records • Neater and legible with less errors.
• Accounts are always up to date.
• Accounts are more acceptable to the guest when totalled and presented.

Time • Most machines have mechanized automatic date printing and abbreviated descriptions of items.
• They have simultaneous preparation of related records.
• They save on labour costs.

When the waiter takes the guest's order for food or beverages, he records it on a triplicate pad; the duplicate copy which goes to the cashier will enable the guest's account to be opened. Thereafter every charge that he incurs during the meal will be recorded by the waiter, who will pass the duplicate copies to the cashier. Each guest's account consists of two parts — the account itself and, attached in front of it, the guest's statement (bill). As charges are made, the two are written up simultaneously and no discrepancies between them are possible. After making each charge the guest's account is balanced automatically. Thus, provided all the vouchers/duplicate orders have been posted, each account is balanced and ready for presentation to the guest.

When the account is paid, the amount paid by the guest is recorded by the machine and the top copy of account (statement) is given to the guest. The second copy is then filed for management control checking.

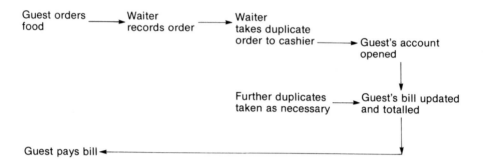

Computerised Control Systems

The system will give financial reports by location and through each cashier or member of staff giving a daily sales analysis and menu item sales.

This system will be linked to the remaining sections of the business, giving a total financial control system for management to use in all outlets.

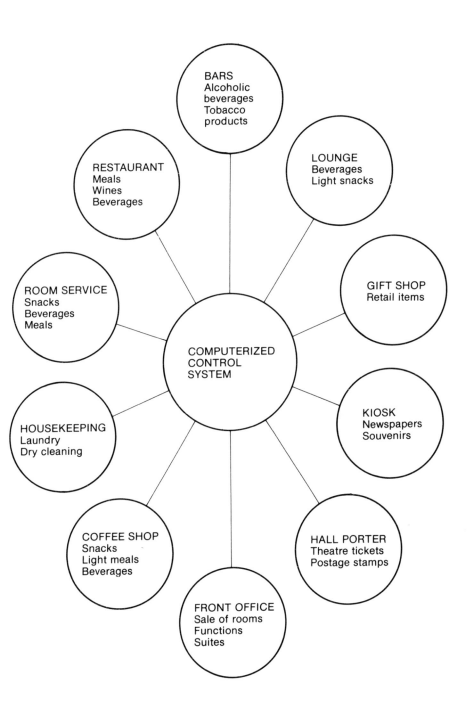

BARS
Alcoholic
beverages
Tobacco
products

LOUNGE
Beverages
Light snacks

RESTAURANT
Meals
Wines
Beverages

GIFT SHOP
Retail items

ROOM SERVICE
Snacks
Beverages
Meals

COMPUTERIZED
CONTROL
SYSTEM

KIOSK
Newspapers
Souvenirs

HOUSEKEEPING
Laundry
Dry cleaning

COFFEE SHOP
Snacks
Light meals
Beverages

HALL PORTER
Theatre tickets
Postage stamps

FRONT OFFICE
Sale of rooms
Functions
Suites

Restaurant and Lounge Control

Terminals are sited in the restaurant, lounge, and bar retail areas, thus making it possible to provide an instant check upon the customer's credit worthiness; charges may then be automatically posted onto the appropriate account.

Action	Control
Guest check is presented for payment	
Guest requests that the bill is placed upon account	Proof required that guest has an account
Guest asked to sign his name and room number on back of check	Proof in case of a query at a later date
Cashier inserts check into terminal till and presses the appropriate key	Terminal memory will recall check total from the original order
Cashier finalises the transaction by activating the charge settlement key	Display reminds cashier to enter guest room number and initials, this confirms the guest's credit worthiness
Cashier checks the display reading of guest's name, room number and amount entered onto that account	
Cashier gives receipt to guest	Amount is posted onto the guest's account.
	Guest checks the receipt with the account before he settles the final amount due

This action occurs at any cash terminal in the premises where a guest wishes to place a charge for goods or services upon his account. It is a very quick and easy system to operate but is expensive to install, and staff have to be adequately trained to use the terminal/tills and to read the data that is produced.

There are many types of system available; they all have the same basic function of accounting for cash and services as they are sold.

Service of Alcoholic Beverages

Aperitifs

These drinks are served before the meal to encourage the digestive system to produce the necessary digestive juices and are usually

194

served in the lounge area or lounge bar. Small dishes of nuts or potato-based snacks are sometimes offered with pre-meal drinks. In the restaurant the customer often likes an aperitif at the table while he is ordering and waiting for his meal. The waiter should therefore ask the host if an appetiser is required as soon as he has seated the party. These should be served as soon as possible, before the order for the meal is taken. The guests may then enjoy their drinks while waiting for their meal.

The following types of aperitif are popular:
- Sherry — served in plain undecorated glasses, often tulip-shaped, narrow at the top and broad at the base.
- Madeira — served in a plain glass of 5–10cl capacity.
- Vermouth — served in a plain glass of average capacity 8–12cl.

Aperitifs are served to the guest in the glass. They should be served from a cloth-covered wine salver in case of slight slipping and spillage. The glass should be placed on the table just below and to the right of the table glass, which should not be removed. If the guests are standing talking at a reception in a lounge area, the waiter should invite them to help themselves to an appetiser from his tray. All empty glasses should be collected during this reception time and ash trays exchanged as soon as they have been used. (See page 199.)

Beer

Bottled beers are usually served in 30cl (½ pint) capacity glasses. Some customers prefer beer to wine to accompany their meal at midday. The waiter should collect the beers from the dispense bar and ensure that they are served to the customer immediately so that the 'head' is still on the top of each glass of beer.

Spirits

These may be requested in the restaurant or lounge area. They are served by standard measure of one-sixth gill, or a double measure one-third gill. Many guests request a particular brand of spirit and if this is not available the waiter should suggest comparable brands. The waiter should obtain the spirits in the glasses, normally of 10–12cl capacity, and any bottles of minerals or mixers requested. He places the glasses on the table and carefully pours a splash of the mixer into the glass. The bottle of mixer should then be placed on the table next to the glass of spirit. Ice should always be available for these drinks.

Wine Storage and Uses

The cellar

- It must be cool and kept at a constant temperature of 12–14°C.
- It should be away from direct sunlight, as strong light can have a harmful effect upon the quality and colour of the wines.
- The cellar must be clean and protected from any strong smelling items, such as fuel or paraffin.
- The wines should be stored horizontally on racks that are not affected by vibrations from traffic or lifts.
- The racks should be labelled or coded to coincide with the wine list numbers to avoid all unnecessary handling or movement of the bottles.

Selling wines in the restaurant

- The wine list should be presented to the host guest and advice given if requested.
- Wines on display must be attractive and labels clearly visible.
- White wines are often sold by the glass from special chilled dispense cabinets.
- Red wines by the glass should be served at room temperature.
- The wines available should meet the needs of the customer.
- A short description of the character of the wines on the wine list will help to increase sales.
- Wine will increase the guests' enjoyment of their meal and for this reason wine sales should be encouraged.

Using wines in the kitchen

- Standard quality wines should be used — never use the dregs of bottles.
- Control of alcohol in the kitchen needs to be strict and constant.
- The wine may be warmed and then flavoured with herbs before being reduced, to concentrate the flavour.
- Convenience wine concentrate is now frequently used to save money and time, as this product is already concentrated and may be added directly into foods. It is easily obtainable in either red or white wine concentrate form.
- The wine should never dominate the flavour of the main foods.

Wine

Wine quality is dependent upon the weather, the quality of the grape harvest, the soil and the skill of the grower. The annual cycle of growing wine is as follows:

Winter — pruning and taking cuttings.

Spring — soil cultivation, spraying plants, weeding.
Summer — spraying plants, protecting grapes from hail and
frost.
Autumn — picking and harvesting the grapes.
A dry year with constant sunshine will produce good quality
vintage wine. A cold spring and wet summer will result in the
grapes having a high acid level and low sugar level.
The flesh of the grape contains water, sugar and acids that are
needed to produce wine; the skins contain the necessary yeast that
causes the juice to ferment.
The conditions that suit the vine best are found in two areas
between 30° and 50° north and south of the Equator. There are
many varieties of vine, the skilled grower will select the type that
suits the soil and climate conditions.
The black grape has the colouring matter in the skin, red wine
may only be made from black grapes; white wine may be made from
black or white grapes.

Wine classification

France
- Vin Ordinaire/Vin de Pays — non-quality wines.
- Vin Délimité de Qualité Supérieure (VDQS) — middle
  quality.
- Appellation d'Origine Contrôlée (AOC) — top quality.

Germany
○ Tafelwein — non-quality wines.
- Qualitalswein-bestimmte-Anbaugebiete (QbA) — ordin-
  ary quality.
- Qualitalswein-mit-Pradehat (QmP) — superior quality.

Italy
- Denominazione d'Origine Controllata (DOC) — quality
  wines.

Methods of Making Wine

White	Red
1. Grapes crushed.	1. Black grapes crushed.
2. Grapes pressed.	2. Grapes into fermenting vat.
3. Juice fermented.	3. Wine run off after 2 weeks.
4. Sweet — fermentation stopped. Dry — fermentation continued. Sparkling — bottled while fermenting.	4. Remaining juice pressed from grapes. Wine and juice blended.

Rosé

1. Black grapes crushed.
2. Grapes into fermenting vat.
3. Pink wine run off after few days.
4. Fermentation continued.

The serving of wine

Bottles of wine are sold to the customer by the wine waiter. A wine list is taken to the host of the group and any advice offered only if requested.

- The chosen wines are presented to the host guest by the wine waiter, with the label uppermost and before being corked.
- Red wine and sweet white wine is then corked and left to breathe until the service time.
- White wine — medium and dry — is corked and placed in an ice bucket to chill prior to service.
- When the wine is to be served the waiter should pour a little 'taste' in the host guest's glass. When this 'taste' has been approved, then the waiter should proceed to serve the guests around the table — taking care never to fill their glasses more than half-full; the host guest should be served last.
- Further wines requested for other courses of the meal should be served in the same manner. Each new wine should be served in a clean glass.

No really hard and fast rules can be drawn up concerning the question of which wines to serve with different courses of a meal. Generally, white wines are served first and with lighter foods such as fish and poultry, and red wines second with meat and game; but the individual preferences of the guests is the most important factor. The following combinations have proved to be popular, however:

Course	Wine
As an aperitif	Dry sherry, dry madeira or champagne
Hors d'oeuvre	Sherry or dry white wine
Oysters	White burgundy, graves, champagne or moselle
Soup	Dry sherry or dry madeira
Fish	White burgundy, graves, champagne, hock, moselle or alsatian
Game and meat	Claret, red burgundy, red rhône wines, or firm-bodied hock
Sweets	Sauternes, barsac, champagne or a rich hock
Cheese	Port, rich sherry, burgundy or hock
Dessert	Port, rich sherry or madeira
Coffee	Brandy or liqueurs

Fortified Wines

A fortified wine is one which has had brandy or some other alcohol added, such as port, sherry, and madeira. The brandy is added to the wine, stops the fermentation process and strengthens the wine. Fortified wines are blended to create an acceptable product that may be either dry or full-bodied and sweet.

Sherry

The best quality sherry comes from the Jerez region of Spain. Other sherries are produced in Australia, South Africa and Cyprus.

Sherry is made from white wine produced from the Palomino grape and the young wine is then lightly fortified. The blending of the sherry is completed using the solera system, which enables a constant taste and colour of any blend to be produced.

Sherry is traditionally served as an aperitif before a meal and helps to stimulate the digestive juices. Pale dry sherries may be served slightly chilled, but sweeter cream sherries should be served at room temperature. Sherry is served in small straight glasses of 4 fl oz capacity.

There are several different types of sherry:
- Fino — Very dry pale sherry. Ideal aperitif.
- Manzanilla — Pale delicate sherry, dry in taste.
- Amontillado — A matured sherry of a dark colour, full sweet flavour.
- Oloroso — A rich dark sweet sherry.
- Milk sherry — A smooth sweet dark-coloured sherry.
- Cream sherry — An older smoother and richer sherry than milk sherry.
- Brown — A dark and sweet type, not as popular as other sherries.

Port

This is produced in the Duoro region of Portugal. The grapes are crushed and fermented and the juice is then blended with brandy. The strengthened wine is blended and matured.

Port is traditionally served at the end of a meal, poured from a decanter into small-sized glasses of 4 fl oz capacity. Port should be served at room temperature.

There are several different types of port:
- Ruby — 4 or 5 years old, a blend of old and new wines.
- Tawny — Matured longer than ruby port and lighter in colour.
- Old tawny — A smooth and matured port of a light colour.
- White port — Made from white grapes, dry, and served as an aperitif.
- Vintage port — Mellow and well matured port, very smooth, it must be decanted.

Beers

Beers are made from barley, yeast, and hops. There are many types of beers, such as pale ale, brown ale, mild and bitter ale and sweet stouts. Recently a lighter beer, known as lager, has grown in popularity. Beers are sold in cans, bottles, or by the pint from draught barrels.

Beer production

1. Malted barley mixed with water — infused at 60°C for 2 hours.
2. Fluid drained off and sugar and hops added — boiled.
3. Liquid cooled to 15°C — yeast added — fermented for 3 days.
4. Surplus yeast skimmed off.
5. Matured for 7 days.
6. Transferred to barrels, tanks, or kegs.
7. Dry hops and dissolved sugar added to improve flavour.
8. Finings added to clarify the beer.
9. Beer is filtered and sampled for quality.

Storage

- Beer should be kept in a well ventilated clean cellar kept at 13°C.
- The cask should be placed on trestles and there it should remain for at least 24 hours to allow it to settle after transportation from the brewery.
- The barrels should be tapped and the spile (wooden peg or spigot) inserted to control the flow of air when the contents are withdrawn.
- All pipes and pumps should be kept absolutely clean to avoid contaminating the beer and so altering the flavour.
- In modern metal kegs the beer is pressurised with carbonic acid (CO_2) to assist the flow of beer.
- Bottled beer should be shelved and allowed to stand for 24 hours to permit it to settle.
- A selection of beers should be placed on the chilled shelf at the end of each service time to ensure that there is an adequate selection of chilled bottled stock ready for the next service time.

Service

- Served in Imperial pint or half pint measures.
- The beer should be carefully poured against the side of the glass to ensure that a small head of froth is created.
- The glasses should be spotlessly clean and care should be taken to ensure that bubbled and dimpled glasses are cleaned between the pattern, as water stains may easily appear on these type of glasses.

Cider

- It is made from apples in the south-west part of England, Devon, Somerset, and Herefordshire.
- The apples are crushed and fermented, then the cider is bottled. It may be either sweet or dry.
- It is served in the same manner as beers and is also available in bottles, cans and on draught.

Spirits

Dispensing spirits

The standard method uses a 10/22 spirit dispenser, which operates on the principle that a known enclosed volume is filled with liquor when one of the changeover action seals releases liquor from the bottle.

But there are problems with this method, such as the following:
- The enclosed volume principle can also trap air, which will affect accuracy.
- The liquor can escape if the seals are not fitted correctly.
- The liquor is dispensed manually, which can cause a spread of bacterial infection.
- Because there is no feedback to the spirit dispenser, control is impossible.

Therefore, an electronic drinks dispenser has been developed to overcome the problems encountered when using the manual spirit dispensers. The equipment makes use of the overflow caused by pushing a plunger down into a reservoir to fill the compartment containing the alcohol to be dispensed. On raising the plunger, surplus liquid flows over the weir back into the first reservoir. In this way the dispensing compartment contains an accurately measured quantity, free from bubbles of air.

The electronic drinks dispenser offers the following features:
- More accuracy — no 'free' drinks, no short measures, no over-measures.
- Fully automatic — dispenses spirits, wines and vermouths.
- Maximum hygiene — no contact with the glass.
- Faster service — fewer staff to serve more customers.
- More security — reduces stock shrinkages with guaranteed measures.
- Microprocessor controlled — automatic stock control reduces high stock levels.
- Attractive finish — will blend into existing bar features.

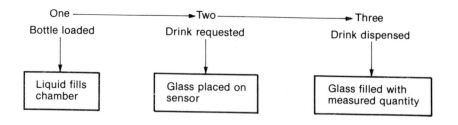

One ─────────────────► Two ─────────────────► Three
Bottle loaded   Drink requested   Drink dispensed

| Liquid fills chamber | | Glass placed on sensor | | Glass filled with measured quantity |

Brandy

- A spirit distilled from wine and matured in wooden casks, where it becomes the characteristic golden colour.
- Bottles of brandy should be stored upright in a mild temperature, between 15°C and 18°C, always away from direct heat and sunlight. This is why the best brandies are found in coloured glass bottles.
- Cognac is a brandy of excellent quality and is produced in a region near the south west of France.
- Brandy is served in specially designed balloon glasses, which enable the full bouquet to be appreciated. The warmth of the hand will encourage the bouquet.

Whisky

- A spirit that is distilled from grain — either barley, rye or maize. Natural pure spring water is a necessary ingredient.
- Malt whisky is made from malted barley. The starch in the grain is turned to sugar, then mixed with the liquid, fermented and distilled.
- Grain whisky is mainly made from maize, with a small proportion of malted barley. It is distilled and matured for at least 3 years, then sent to be blended.
- Blended Scotch whisky is a mix of 60 per cent grain and 40 per cent malt and is blended using whisky of different ages and origins to produce the required taste.
- Deluxe Scotch whiskies are older and more mellow in flavour; they are smooth whiskies that have been matured for at least 7 years, some for as many as 12 years.
- Whisky is served in one-sixth gill measures and may be drunk neat, with ice when it is known as 'on the rocks', or sometimes with a mixer, such as dry ginger.
- Malt and deluxe Scotch whiskies are drunk neat in straight or cut-glass spirit tumblers.

Rum

- A spirit that is distilled from sugar cane in the Caribbean, Jamaica, Guyana, Trinidad, and Barbados.
- Rum may be a dark, rich, highly-flavoured spirit, which can be used in cakes, Christmas puddings and mincemeat, fruit babas, and other sweets. It used to be drunk daily by the Royal Navy as their rum ration.
- Bacardi rum is a clear light spirit without the highly flavoured taste of the dark rum. This light rum is served with fruit drinks and ice.
- Rum is served in one-sixth gill measures.

Gin

- A spirit made with grain and molasses and flavoured with juniper berries and coriander seeds.
- London gin is made by re-distilling a neutral spirit with flavourings; it may be clear or straw coloured.
- Plymouth gin is distilled in Plymouth; it has a unique flavour.
- Gin is served in one-sixth gill measures, often with a tonic water or fruit juice to flavour and create a long drink.

Vodka

- Distilled from grain or molasses and is a pure spirit with no flavourings added.
- As a tasteless spirit it may be mixed with any fruit-based juice or mineral water.
- Served in one-sixth gill measure and in a tall glass to create a long drink.

Liqueurs

These are spirits flavoured with fruits and herbs, roots, and plants, and sometimes sweetened or blended.

A liqueur is served after the meal has been completed, in a small size glass of 2.5cl capacity. Liqueurs are served from a liqueur trolley and offered to the guests to accompany their after dinner coffee. Small mint chocolates are also offered at the end of a dinner and these sometimes replace the liqueurs.

There are many different types of liqueurs:

- Advocaat — thick, yellow, and creamy; made from eggs and spirits.
- Apricot brandy — a mix of apricots and brandy.
- Chartreuse — green or yellow distilled brandy and herbs.

- Cherry brandy — a mix of cherries and brandy.
- Cointreau — orange flavoured colourless spirit.
- Crème de menthe — a liqueur flavoured with mint leaves.
- Curaçao — a spirit distilled from orange peel; it may be coloured blue for cocktails.
- Drambuie — Scotch whisky and herbs blended with honey.
- Grand Marnier — a mix of oranges and cognac.
- Irish Cream — cream and whisky blended with a trace of chocolate.
- Irish Mist — heather honey and whisky blended together.
- Maraschino — a sweet liqueur made from cherries.
- Tia Maria — distilled from sugar cane and coffee.

Unit 10 Assessment Activities

1. (a) Make a collection of menus from any establishments that you have visited.
   (b) With each menu write notes on: the type of establishment; the style of service; the method used to pay for it.
   (c) Display your collection and the adjacent notes.

2. (a) Draw a flow chart to illustrate the restaurant control system in your place of work or study.
   (b) Discuss its merits and make any recommendations for change that you consider might be advantageous.

3. (a) Make a collection of labels from one type of alcoholic drink.
   (b) Compare the differences between the contents of the bottles in relation to the: cost; taste; method of service; and method of manufacture.

4. (a) Draw the glasses used at your place of work and indicate which types of alcoholic drinks are served in each sized glass.
   (b) Indicate how glasses should be handled and cleaned to eliminate the risks of cross infection.

5. (a) Write a cleaning schedule for a lounge bar, to include the bar itself and the lounge area for the members of the general public.
   (b) Indicate the areas that will need extra attention to prevent the risk of cross infection.

Index

CATERING: HOUSEKEEPING & FRONT OFFICE

Ursula Jones

As a basic theory guide to housekeeping and front office skills, this book gives straightforward, easily-understood explanations of the main principles involved. Wherever possible, material is presented in tabular form for ease of assimilation by students. Helpful illustrations of specific equipment and methods are also provided throughout, and each unit is followed by questions in the form of assessment activities.
Contents include:

* types of residential establishment and staffing structures
* cleaning systems and equipment
* cleaning agents and methods
* house services control
* hotel reception
* management, organisation and business affairs

Catering students who are to be examined by the City and Guilds London Institute will find the contents of this book relevant to examinations 705, 708, 709 and the 700 skills series. Trainees on HCITB and YTS schemes will also find it helpful, as will those on TVEI and CPVE courses.

The following books are also available from:

Edward Arnold (Publishers) Ltd
41 Bedford Square
London WC1B 3DQ

BASIC CATERING ASSIGNMENTS

Richard Sharpe, Janet Sharpe and David Sullivan

A book of integrated assignments covering the core objectives of prevocational schemes related to the hotel, catering and tourism industries.

* All situations are realistic and drawn from the authors' wide experience of industry and training
* The assignments aim to challenge students and to stimulate interest by involving them in their own learning. Each section begins with a full list of the objectives covered.
* The assignments exercise a full range of skills in communication, industrial and craft knowledge, numeracy and work and life skills.
* The skills covered in each assignment are transferable to a wide range of work situations.
* Basic background information is supplied in each section.
* The book is heavily illustrated with realistic documents, photographs and line drawings.

PRACTICAL COOKERY Fifth Edition

Victor Ceserani & Ronald Kinton

The fifth edition of this well-known book designed to provide a sound foundation in professional cookery, takes into account the recent changes and revisions of catering schemes and the related examinations by providing general and specific learning objectives for each chapter. The authors have updated the content to reflect current practice in education and the trade. The text has been carefully reset and the index completely revised and simplified.

THE THEORY OF CATERING Fifth Edition

Ronald Kinton & Victor Ceserani

This book's simple and practical treatment of hygiene, nutrition, commodities, and preservation, as well as its wealth of detail about professional catering operations make it useful both as a text and as an introduction for those students who are considering careers in the trade.

FOOD AND BEVERAGE SERVICE Second Edition

D R Lillicrap

The contents of this illustrated book lead from the basic principles involved in food and beverage service to the more advanced techniques of banqueting organisation and administration; basic drink service and the service of wines.

THE SCIENCE OF CATERING

J A Stretch & H A Southgate

A comprehensive text covering the background science of all aspects of the catering industry. The book is written in readily understandable English and any scientific terms used are defined in the text and in the glossary provided at the end of the book. Further explanation is provided by the large number of line illustrations and photographs. Each chapter starts with a brief summary of its objectives, and self-assessment or multiple choice questions are provided at the end of each topic.

HOTEL RECEPTION Fourth Edition

P B White & H Beckley

The new edition of this popular text takes into account the changing nature of hotel reception in terms of practice and new technology. It includes new photographs, drawings and documents and the text has been completely updated and new chapters on sales, security and computers have been added.

HOTEL, HOSTEL AND HOSPITAL HOUSEKEEPING
Fourth Edition

J C Branson & M Lennox

This text will give students an appreciation of the technical skills involved in working in an accomodation services department as well as an understanding of management. It will be of interest to those intending to enter the industry as well as those already on courses.

Please write for our full catalogue of catering and hotelkeeping titles.